A WALK IN OLD SYDNEY

A WALK IN OLD SYDNEY

MICHAEL TATLOW

NEW
HOLLAND

Contents

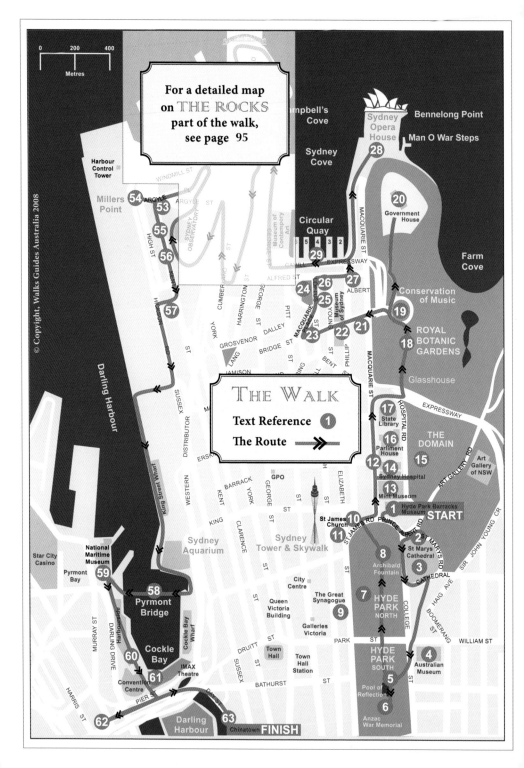

The Walk

OUR RECOMMENDED TOUR of exploration takes you to the scenes of Sydney's astonishing past, warts and all. We visit its most historic districts from the top of old Macquarie Street to Circular Quay, all over The Rocks, then south to Darling Harbour. Along the way, we present several Snapshots, reliving dramatic and funny moments in Old Sydney and presenting some of its extraordinary characters.

You can do our walk in a casual few hours but to soak up the heritage of Sydney, to reflect on those heady and horrific days and to spend time in at least some of the scrumptious diversity of shops, restaurants, pubs and attractions along the way, why not make it a day or more of revelations? Enjoy!

Possession of a continent. An idealised image of the Flag of Queen Anne above Captain Phillip and his officers at Sydney Cove, 26 January 1788, claiming Australia for England. By Algernon Talmage. Mitchell Library, State Library of NSW.

The Birth of Sydney

IMAGINE THE BEWILDERMENT and panic of Sydney if one sunny afternoon a flotilla of ships from outer space lobbed on the Harbour and their strangely-coloured occupants in weird costumes and speaking in an alien tongue came ashore carrying weapons of terror and claimed this land for themselves.

That sort of spectacle confronted the Cadigal people of Aborigines who had lived here, unchanged for some 40,000 years when in January 1788 a convoy of 11 sailing ships gathered in a pristine inlet teeming with fish, the shore thick with oysters and mussels and trees. Over several hot days 1,483 men, women and children came ashore. Also astonishing to the eyes of the natives were 500 unimagined animals; horses, goats, cattle, sheep, pigs, turkeys, geese, ducks, chooks and, ominously, rabbits.

Also dogs of strange colours and shapes, so different from the dingos Aborigines had kept for millennia. The natives never interfered with the animals. They were not interested in eating such weird creatures.

The settlers were similarly intrigued by the seemingly-timid black and naked residents of this land, the hopping animal the kangaroo, gigantic fowls (emus) the Cadigals called marayong, gum trees with trunks of ghostly white and scavenging black crows that squawked like harbingers of doom. Even the abounding swans were black instead of the white ones of England. Shrieks from cockatoos of white under crests of yellow rent the firmament. What monsters, the newcomers wondered, lurked in the forested wilderness of the harbour's northern shore?

Cadigals watched from the bushes in awe as men in red jackets and white britches and a variety of strange head gear gathered above the little beach at the cove and raised a flag of red, white and blue by a casuarina tree and a wiry little man with a long nose in the most elaborate outfit of all claimed this land in the name of the King of England. The natives quaked as the Red Coats blasted a volley of shots into thundering clouds from muskets that belched smoke.

Pioneer explorers on the North Shore overlooking Sydney Cove about 1845. Artist G.E. Peacock. Mitchell Library, State Library of NSW.

The Cadigals had 15 other clans in today's Sydney region. They were even more perplexed by the customs of these aliens a month later when a convict, Thomas Barrett, stealer of beef and peas, was strung up from a tree in front of the whole white population and hanged.

Sydney's old coat of arms.

The man in the finery at the flag raising was Captain Arthur Phillip, leader of the First Fleet and the penal colony's first Governor. He had chosen deep and sheltered Sydney Cove (now Circular Quay) with a handy stream of water for the first settlement of whites in Australia after astutely rejecting a site south in Botany Bay that London had recommended. The settlement for a while was called Albion, the ancient Roman name for Britain. As usual with early explorers, Phillip had named the cove after his boss, Lord Sydney (Thomas Townsend) the Secretary of State for Home Affairs in London. Sydney was then adopted as the name for the settlement.

After losing the War of Independence against America, England had suddenly needed a new and remote place to dump thousands of people crammed into its jails and prison hulks on the river Thames in grimy old London. So the government decided to assume ownership of the mysterious continent at the ends of the earth for its convicts, most of them imprisoned by shamefully-harsh laws to protect the property of the upper classes.

Laws that later transported Tom Rares, aged nine, to seven years of cruel incarceration in the colony for stealing an apple. After seven years, this child of the London slums was told he faced another seven in custody. He escaped the next day and went bushranging. Tom Rares was caught, badly wounded and, still semi-conscious, hanged at the age of 16…laws that had Mary Reibey, aged 14, given the same sentence in England for riding a horse without the permission of its owner, her neighbour. Few child convicts returned to their families but at least unsinkable Mary prospered so in Sydney that she is pictured on today's Australian $20 note.

Six of the First Fleet's ships landed cargoes of 732 convicts after a voyage via South America and South Africa lasting eight months and a week. One hundred and eighty nine of the convicts were women with 12 babes and 14 were children. Several soldiers' wives and convicts bore children on the voyage and about 22 prisoners died. Two hundred and forty five Royal Marines landed to guard the convicts. The marines brought 31 wives and 11 children.

Phillip sent the convicts to pitch tents under guard on the steep and rocky western shore of the cove, now The Rocks. The more-fertile land east of the sweet and trickling stream that flowed to the cove was set aside for administrators' and free settlers' huts and tents, for grazing the farm animals and planting vegetables and grain seeds. Also here was the Governor's portable Government House of canvas and his greyhounds.

The Pacific Ocean region was the least known and least regarded part of the world to Europeans at the time. Apart from some explorers in the previous 200 or so years, only opportunistic killers of whales and seals had come this way. The Spanish still ran California and Mexico. China and Japan, old though their cultures were, still lived in feudal times. Few Pacific Islanders had seen a white man.

The soldiers in Sydney soon refused to guard the wretched but bawdy convicts at their camp of squalor among the rocks, forcing Phillip to appoint convict overseers. Twenty years later, the NSW Corps became the colony's crooked traders of imported rum, which was used as currency. They led Australia's first and only political coup, the Rum Rebellion, arresting and deposing the Governor of the day, William Bligh; a sound administrator and former victim of the Bounty mutiny who challenged the merchants' corruption.

With a few bloody exceptions, the first whites here related pretty well with the Aborigines. Whites who harmed Aborigines were punished as were natives who sometimes attacked whites, usually in retaliation against stealers of their possessions, like bark canoes.

For quite a while, the new nation nearly starved to death; getting shipments of mostly more convicts from an England more interested in exporting law breakers and fighting the French than feeding this antipodean outpost. Over 80 years, 158,829 convicts were banished to Australia. Some were real crooks

The emerging Sydney in about the 1820s. This unsigned etching looks south-east across the Cove from the top of The Rocks. The large building across the water, above a garden, was the first Government House. Mitchell Library, State Library of NSW.

Sydney Cove from the North Shore in 1825, 37 years after white settlement. The new spire of St. James Church is on the left. Right, Flagstaff Hill, behind the Dawes point Battery. Joseph Lycett painting, Dixon Galleries, State Library of NSW.

but some were political exiles from Ireland, Canada, New Zealand and even America who opposed British occupation.

The settlement lurched along, with outposts claimed at the South Pacific's Norfolk Island and on Van Diemen's Land (now Tasmania) by 1803. The major export for years was seal skins for China.

Thanks to the indomitable spirit of men and women that characterises so many of today's Australians, the penal colony's plagues and famines were overcome, and farm and then manufacturing production gradually rose. Sydney was declared a city with a mayor and aldermen in 1842. Australia had become a self-sustaining, nearly booming country, even sending young men to make war for England, by the time it was federated into a nation of States in 1901.

Clogged here and there as it is today in its booming bustle, in streets in the inner city formed from unplanned walking and bullock wagon tracks, Sydney is still the hub of the nation; a multicultural metropolis with restaurants specialising in dishes of nearly every land. It enjoys sparkling harbours and estuaries, is nourished by many streams, with magnificent beaches to the east and brooded over from the west by mountains of blue.

We hope these pages show you how the rough and ragged colony of mostly convicts and their keepers has evolved in only 223 years into the wondrous place that spawned a nation. It is Australia's biggest city in a setting and climate the envy of most of the world. Its four and a half million residents

are immigrants and descendants of settlers from all parts of the world and also urbanised Aborigines from all over the island continent; more than lived here when Governor Phillip and company arrived to bewilder the Cadigals.

The banksia,
Sydney's official flower

A WALK IN OLD SYDNEY

Sydney Cove in 1788, a few weeks after white settlement. Mitchell Library, State Library of NSW.

Hyde Park Barracks, Courtesy Historic Houses Trust NSW

Part One

Hyde Park Barracks, St Marys,
Australian Museum, St James

AS MARKED on the map, A Walk in Old Sydney takes a route in the general shape of an inverted horseshoe through the heart of the city's colonial heritage, with its reminders of dramatic moments and characters.

From the end of the right arm at the top of Macquarie Street, we loop south to discover some old tales of St Marys Cathedral, the Australian Museum and Hyde Park. Our Walk then goes north via Bridge Street to Circular Quay and The Rocks at the top arc of the horseshoe. We then explore the historic colour of Millers Point and complete our amble south to Darling Harbour and Chinatown. Apart from some steep and staired spots at The Rocks and a couple of other places that can be bypassed, the Walk is wheelchair friendly. So, let's go!

1 The ideal place to begin the Walk is at the top of Macquarie Street, the city's first grand avenue and still its most elegant. The place to meet your fellow strollers and get a good grounding on Sydney's heritage is at the World Heritage listed **Hyde Park Barracks**, in Macquarie Street just north of Hyde Park. Mayhem reigned in the dark lanes and shanties of Sydney in the early 1800s, thanks to a government that ladled basic food to its convicts, worked them from dawn until dusk but did not provide lodgings. Penniless felons ranged widely at night, stealing grog, food, clothes and money, and slept in alleys and shrubbery.

Queens Square and the Hyde Park Barracks in 1836. Painted by Robert Russell. Mitchell Library, State Library of NSW.

Desperate men and women convicts, virtual slaves who built the settlement's infrastructure and buildings and did work the free settlers eschewed, would fight to the death for sleeping rights to a cosy spot in a stable. The soldiers, themselves a corruption-led rabble, had long abandoned most attempts in parts of Sydney to enforce the colony's harsh laws.

Francis Greenway

New Governor Lachlan Macquarie decided to ease the sleaze by commissioning architect Francis Greenway, a convict transported for forging a work contract, to design a dormitory to which the settlement's 1,000 and more vagrant male prisoners would have to retire at night. With delicious irony, the forger was pictured on Australia's first $10 note. He was the colony's first architect.

It could have looked like a big barn at the top of the thoroughfare the governor had named after himself. But the result was the Barracks, a masterpiece of classic Georgian simplicity, the gem of Greenway's many buildings that gave a character of grace to Old Sydney. Originally called the Convict Barracks, it was nothing flash, like the Gothic and Italianate edifices we will see along the way. Largely unskilled convicts with limited tools built the Barracks on a low budget from 1817 to 1819 of mellow sandstock bricks with an arched entrance and lower front windows. Convict clockmaker James Oatley installed the clock (made by Benjamin Vuillamy) inside the front Grecian gable.

The convicts slept in an upstairs dormitory in serried hammocks that enclosed them like sausage skins. Convict boys slept in a separate dormitory for a few years until they were moved to another place. Those caught for offences including drunkenness, gambling, being cheeky to the guards, feigning illnesses or not returning to the Barracks at night were sent to a treadmill or flogged with up to 50 lashes from a flesh-ripping whip near the Barracks' rear wall. They were marched, many in leg irons, four abreast in their clothes of yellow canvas branded with broad arrow marks or HPD (for Hyde Park

Barracks) to and from work on projects like carving the Argyle Cut at The Rocks and toiling up to their waists in slime reclaiming Sydney Cove to form Circular Quay.

Wealthy persons of influence who had moved into plush townhouses in Macquarie Street included John Fairfax and Charles Kemp, co-owners of *The Sydney Morning Herald*. They pressured the administration to end the presence of convicts in their enclave. And it seems the governor obliged.

At the time, the colony had a serious shortage of women. Thousands of single girls, many fleeing the potato famine in Ireland, responded to a migration program promising them work in the antipodes. They came here by the shipload for nearly 40 years from 1848. Convict transportation to NSW had officially ended, although four shiploads came in 1849 amid uproar from the Anti-Transportation League. The governor moved the girls into the Barracks. The convict men were sent to the secure isolation of Cockatoo Island in the Harbour. The women were employed mostly as maid servants under the caring eye of their champion, Caroline Chisholm. Lots of the girls, of course, married. The austere Australian Monument to the Great Irish Famine is by the Barracks' south wall. It is a regular meeting place for Australians of Irish extraction. Caroline Chisholm, women and children and scenes of Old Sydney were pictured on Australia's first $5 note. She was the first woman so honoured on our currency apart from monarchs.

The Barrack's top floor was an asylum for 200 to 300 destitute women from 1862 to 1884. The Immigration Depot here for seven years to 1855 housed wives and children of convicts reuniting with their husbands and fathers. Then the NSW Department of Justice took over the building, dividing it into court rooms and offices.

A major restoration for nine years from 1975 saw the demolition of a cacophony of ramshackle buildings attached to the Barracks over the years to restore the purity of Greenway's gem we see today.

The life of the Barracks has been in four phases: a keeper of convicts from 1819 to 1848, an immigration depot and asylum from 1848 to 1886, law courts and government offices from 1887 to 1979, when it was restored and turned into today's museum of its own past. The ground floor has a fine book and

A gang of convicts at Hyde Park Barracks in 1830. Like many 19th century works, this unfairly depicts convicts as ugly brutes. Broad arrows on their clothes and all sorts of equipment showed that it was government property. Augustus Earle's lithograph The Jail Gang (Views in NSW 1830). Mitchell Library, State Library of NSW.

souvenir shop and information desk, a collection of artifacts and an extensive Greenway Gallery. A café is in the grounds north of the main building. The second level is devoted to collections about the Barracks' events, people and archaeology. It includes some 85,000 items recovered from the grounds and under floorboards. The top level has been restored to the way convicts had originally built it.

There is a section about characters of the Barracks over the years and don't miss a reconstruction of the huge dormitory of convicts' hammocks complete with recorded sounds of those days from 1819 to 1848. School children and scouting groups can be colonial felons for a night by booking a hammock followed by a basic breakfast. Rats no longer flourish in the place, we're assured.

SNAPSHOT 1833
A flash new lash: Hyde Park Barracks

THE CAT-O-NINE-TAILS swished through the air and into his back. The shock made the convict gasp for air between clenched teeth. He didn't think it would be like this! His back was scarred from many past floggings, but this time it was different. Superintendent Ernest Augustus Slade was right, his newly-designed "cat" was vicious.

Slade was appointed Superintendent of the Barracks in February 1833. And so began his 20-month reign of callous brutality. The convicts hated him. Slade was enormously proud of his new "regulation lash" with its longer handle and knotted cords. When giving evidence to the Select Committee on Transportation in England in 1837, he told the Lords, "… 50 lashes under my superintendence was equal to 1,000 under any other man's ever before in the colony".

Slade relished his job. On 29 August 1833, the Colonial Secretary sent a memo to superintendents and magistrates requiring them to personally administer all corporal punishments. They were also asked to furnish reports describing every punishment inflicted in the following month. Slade's descriptions are astonishing. He recorded in minute detail the sufferings of each of the 52 convicts flogged between September 4 and 30. In some cases, he noted that particular convicts had been sufficiently punished by the half way point, but that did not stop the convict from receiving his full quota of 50 lashes. The Governor, Sir Richard Bourke, was responsible for ending Slade's career. The boss of the Barracks was living with a young girl who had just borne his daughter when he procured a newly-arrived lass, Lavinia Winter, as a servant. Some concerned people felt that he had procured Lavinia for prostitution. A resulting court case caused quite a scandal in Old Sydney. Sir Richard Bourke asked for Slade the sadist's resignation.

After his departure his new "regulation" cat-o-nine-tails was still used for punishment. Other torture included solitary confinement, working in irons or the treadmill. A treadmill was at Carters Barracks, near where Central Railway now stands. Convicts sentenced to the treadmill were marched to it every day for their punishment. It had slats or steps around a large wooden cylinder that revolved, like a never-ending staircase, as the line of men trod on the next step. The convicts in coarse trousers and little or no underclothes christened this abysmal machine the 'cock-chafer'.

FROM THE BARRACKS, we recommend a short loop of revelations to the left before our stroll along Macquarie Street. Go to Prince Albert Road and past the ornate stone Lands Titles Office building.

2 On an island at the junction with Art Gallery Road, heading to the Art Gallery of NSW in the Domain, is a grandiose monument dedicated to **Aquarius** and **Arethusa**, ancient Greek myth characters relating to water. Grazier and politician John Frazer presented it to the community in 1884.

3 Frazer's pagan shrine must have galled its neighbours across the street at **St Marys Cathedral**, already miffed at Governor Macquarie since 1821 for plonking them on a site so near the Hyde Park Barracks of convicts. We will soon see another pagan jibe at the cathedral, from Hyde Park on its western flank.

Many of the famous and infamous folk of modern and Old Sydney have been 'matched and despatched' at this enormous Gothic Revival centre of Catholic life in the nation in College Street. Architect William Wardell designed it based on Notre Dame in Paris and England's Lincoln Cathedral.

Catholics predominated in colonial Sydney, in number but not in power, thanks to convict transportation and emigration from Ireland. The priests first built a modest Catholic chapel here. It was destroyed by fire in 1865. Work on the cathedral began in 1868 and it was dedicated 14 years later. The spires planned for the southern towers were finally placed in 1999 to herald the 21st century.

The statues by the steps at the cathedral's southern grand entrance are of Archbishop Dr Michael Kelly and Cardinal Francis Patrick Moran, sculpted by Sir Bertram Mackennal. Do go inside this impressive structure to experience an ethereal aura of muted light shafting from on high through thick and brightly-stained windows to a medieval crypt. The nation's largest mosaic in the floor of the crypt makes a brilliant course to the sanctuary. It is of Celtic enamelwork in scarlet, greens and blues depicting the six days of creation. The terrazzo mosaic is a masterpiece by Peter Melocco. There are guided tours of St Marys, which of course has a shop.

St Marys Cathedral.

This ornate monument to Roman pagan myth heroes Aquarius and Arethusa must have irked the priests at nearby St Marys Cathedral when it was installed in 1821.

As we leave the cathedral, facing an area popular with skate-boarders, go left down the stone steps and turn right into the peaceful splendour of Cook and Phillip Park. It is named of course to honour Captain James Cook, pioneer explorer of Australia's east coast, and Sydney's first governor, Arthur Phillip.

A path takes us south through this oasis of mature trees, shrubs, flowers and lawns to the left and, right, the park's Aquatic and Fitness Centre.

We will see a lot more of these graceful old Moreton Bay fig trees during our Walk.

Nearing William Street the path runs beside an area studded heavily with trees to form a dense canopy, in turn creating a dappled sanctuary, a patch of tropical forest, in the heart of the nation's biggest city. It is a preserve of fossicking ibis whenever your author goes there. We are likely to see more of these big birds. When the ibis came to town in big numbers some years ago, they forced the Council to enclose the tops of the city's rubbish bins. Ibis used to perch on the edge of the old open-top bins and, using their long and curved beaks, scatter rubbish all over the ground. Scavenging seagulls followed the ibis everywhere. This park is the first of several magnificently-kept reserves on our Walk; thanks to the City of Sydney Council.

4 Cross William Street, which goes east to Kings Cross, at the College Street lights to enter one of the finest natural history museums in the world, the **Australian Museum**. It takes hours properly to explore this house of natural treasures.

It is the very best place to find out about the nation's zoology, botany, anthropology, pre-history, minerals and geology. Also the history of Aborigines, Melanesians even Eskimos and Egyptians. The skeleton of a 20- metre sperm whale found dead on a beach near Wollongong in 1871 hangs over the entrance foyer. It has been there since 1910. A café is to the left and, right, is an excellent shop selling books, souvenirs and toys that include stuffed kangaroos, wombats and Tasmanian tigers made in, yes, China. Upstairs are skeletons, fossils and other relics from the island continent's prehistory. Remains and recreations of dinosaurs abound here. Elsewhere there are (phony) nuggets of gold, specimens of opals and diamonds, and the skeleton of a giant eastern grey kangaroo.

The original building, designed by colonial Architect Mortimer Lewis, opened in 1857. The College Street Palladian wings and front were the first assignment for James Barnet, who replaced a sacked Lewis in 1849. Walter McGill carved the Corinthian pillars at the main façade.

A forested sanctuary for timid animals in the heart of the city at Cook and Phillip Park.

5 Cross William Street to take the steps to the southern half of **Hyde Park,** a haven of greenery the size a few big city blocks where we are welcomed by a giant, waving statue of Captain Cook. Immigrant Englishman Thomas Woolner sculpted it in 1879.

6 Take the elevated path west beside Park Street to the long boulevard bordered by trees leading left to the **Anzac Memorial**. The shrine built in 1934 to Australians killed in World War I is now a memorial to all who served their country at war. The memorial has an *Australians at War* photographic exhibition and a circular Hall of Memory. The memorial brings big crowds to services on Anzac Day. Groups of mostly ex-servicemen then disperse around Hyde Park, with popular two-up gambling legalised there on that one day of the year.

7 The boulevard continues north across Park Street to enter perhaps the most tale-riddled piece of turf in Australia. **Hyde Park, North** is an old and august oasis of greenery embowered by the city. The whole park was declared a public common, to be a sort of giant village green, in 1792 when Sydney was little more than a collection of huts and tents.

The whole area of today's park was a swampy heath, abundant with ducks, swans, water hens and water rats that were hunted by Aborigines. It drained into the ferny and timbered gully of the Tank Stream, about where Pitt Street is today. The rivulet enticed the First Fleeters to settle at Sydney Cove. With remarkable foresight, Governor Phillip declared today's park "a common, never to be granted or leased". By the time Governor Macquarie arrived in 1810, the reserve had taken on an oval shape known as the Racecourse. Never one to respect popular place naming, Macquarie in 1810 dubbed the area Hyde Park after the park in London. His proclamation said: "The whole of the open Ground yet unoccupied in the Vicinity of the Town of Sydney, hitherto known and alternately called the Common, Exercising Ground, Cricket Ground and Race Course ... [is] intended in future for the Recreation and Amusement of the Inhabitants of the Town, and as a Field of Exercise for the Troops". It has not been repealed, so it seems that

A reverential crowd around the Pool of Remembrance at the unveiling of the War Memorial, Hyde Park, in November 1934. Holtermann Collection, State Library NSW.

troops can still exercise there. Convicts under Macquarie's Scots troops drained, cleared and levelled the land to form a racecourse a kilometre long.

They posted another proclamation: 'No Gaming, Drunkenness, Swearing, Quarrelling, Boxing, Cows or Goats Pastured, no Pie Selling, no erection of Booths for the sale of Liquor.' So watch it! No quarrelling. Constables carried off offenders. They faced jail, the treadmill or the public pillories and stocks, abused and pelted at with rotten fruit, as convicts looked on from the upper windows of Hyde Park Barracks. Your author, who likes a tipple and lively discussion and has pastured goats, is relieved to understand that the whole proclamation is not enforced in modern Sydney. But, I have noted, a sign by the northern end of the park across St James Road still enforces some of Macquarie's edicts. No drinking or carrying of alcohol or "pursuing business", for instance, is allowed.

The first game of cricket in Australia was played in 1803 at the future park, then a swampy pasture where sheep grazed. It was between a scratch team (gentlemen only) of locals and officers from HMS Calcutta, which had brought convicts and settlers from England to Van Diemen's Land (now Tasmania). After the game, players and supporters gathered at Tunks Hotel, at the corner of (now) Elizabeth and Park streets.

The Sydney Morning Herald reported an elite episode of "the noble, manly and scientific game of cricket" at the Old Race Course in 1832. The winners got a purse of £25, a year's pay then for a labourer. The new Australia Cricket Club and the Amateur Society pitched their tents under the clubs' imperial flags before play. They and friends retired to the tents (after the Australia Club won by 20 runs) where "a capital repast was spread". Cricket later moved to the Domain.

The first race meeting here, a grand three-day affair in October 1810, heralded today's Spring Racing Carnival. Jockeys mounted on the call of a bugle and raced on the shot of a musket. Despite Sydney's general poverty, horse-racing society was well rewarded with winners getting 50 guineas (£55). Races were run clockwise, as they still are in NSW. Said society danced and drank through the night at a grand ball to end that maiden horse racing carnival.

The '"manly" game of cricket, Hyde Park, 27 October 1843, between Sydney civilians and the Imperial Regiment. Left, Elizabeth Street. Centre, St James Church. Right, Hyde Park Barracks and the future College Street. Dixson Galleries, State Library of NSW.

8 We recommend a rest by the glistening **Archibald Fountain** amid the trees, the focus of the park, to contemplate on some of the things and past events around here. The bronze statuary, by the way, was a gift to the city by a founder of *The Bulletin* magazine, J. F. Archibald (1856-1919) to commemorate the bonds between Australia and France during World War I. It is the work of French artist Francois Sicard.

Apollo, the ancient Greek god of the sun, towers over Diana the Roman huntress with her bow as Greek myth's Theseus slays the minotaur. Your author suspects that it is no coincidence that Apollo the pagan was placed extending an arm provocatively towards St Marys Cathedral. In December 1878, a raging rabble of 10,000 racists ranted at Hyde Park against Chinese coming to Australia, bringing Oriental customs they feared, discovering gold the mob reckoned they would have found. Thugs left the park in the night to assault Chinese people around the town and stone and burn their premises. Families without homes or work during the Depression around 1930 pitched tents in Hyde Park until they were moved on to the Domain.

In the park's north-west corner near St James Road and Elizabeth Street is a little fountain that spills water to a sort of stairway of four shallow dishes of conglomerated stone. John Byrom designed this quaint lot in 1962 to commemorate the end location near here of Busby's Bore, Sydney's first supply of piped water for 22 years from 1837. A stone tunnel, which is still there, delivered the goods from now-Centennial Park 3.6 km away. It was the work of convicts and engineer John Busby. Carters lined up by wooden trestles and sold water around town by the bucket load. For a while, it was planned to quench the settlement's thirst from a huge, a 60-million-litre, reservoir convicts were going to dig in the park!

But in colonial times this former marsh and racetrack was mostly a place to promenade in your finery, to be seen and gossip and relax and picnic on the grass amid trees and flowers, imported mostly (regrettably, I reckon) from other countries.

8

The superb Archibald Fountain.
Is Apollo the pagan god goading St Marys?

9 The **Great Synagogue**, the Australian centre of the Jewish faith. Built in 1878, it overlooks Hyde Park from Elizabeth Street north of Park Street. The magnificent building of moulded and carved sandstone quarried at Pyrmont looks awfully cramped between high, modern boxes. Thomas Rowe designed the synagogue, which seats 1,600 on the ground level, in the Byzantine style of synagogues in England. There are public tours from its Elizabeth Street side on Tuesdays and Thursdays. The building is an enchantment of sumptuousness amid columns of cast iron, arches of plaster and stained-glass windows.

Leave Hyde Park from its northern end. A safe way to cross busy St James Road is through an underground tunnel that is part of the St James railway station. We emerge at Queens Square, near a big, mounted statue of a snooty-looking Queen Victoria looking down Macquarie Street from where there was once a fine view of Sydney Harbour. The statue was moved from today's Botanic Gardens to here in 1881. She is placed to ignore the statue of her consort, Prince Albert, facing her across the street.

St James Church in 1836. By Robert Russell. Mitchell Library, State Library of NSW.

10 Sydney, by the way, is riddled with old tunnels, carved by convicts for people, water supplies and sewerage. A network of them, long disused, connected Hyde Park Barracks with **St James Church** before us and the law courts so convicts had little chance of scarpering when going to and from church services and facing bewigged dispensers of the rough justice of the time.

Built from 1820, St James is Sydney's oldest standing church. Another product from architect Francis Greenway, it was intended to be a courthouse. Now overshadowed by modern high-rise blocks, the Anglican church was to be the western elegance of an immense and open Queens Square at the top of Macquarie Street, facing the Hyde Park Barracks. But, many refurbishings later, its colonial Georgian style, its mellow stone façade and classical stone porch at the top of King Street make St James a gem in the concrete jungle. Its first slender spire of copper sheets, marked with government-property broad arrows to deter thieves, was a landmark for ships in the harbour before the high-rise boom.

Today's spire of green sheathing and its cross were erected in 1894. Its designer was Varney Parkes. He was a son of Sir Henry Parkes, five times Premier of NSW and Father of the Federation of the colonies in 1901 who founded what he called the Commonwealth of Australia.

The church's nave and semicircular sanctuary rest on a stone-vaulted crypt. It has a shop and, if you are looking for local ancestors, the crypt stores stacks of ledgers recording baptisms, marriages and funerals held in the church. Robed lawyers attend special services at St James in January to mark the beginning of law terms.

11 As we face St James, to the left bordering St James Road and behind a high fence, is a little garden of flowers, shrubs and cosy benches on a lawn – the exclusive domain, we understand, of judges and others of the legal profession, when determining decisions for the adjoining **Supreme Court of NSW**. The wall of the building has a coat of arms carved in stone in 1895 of the British lion and what looks more like a horse than a unicorn.

Going back towards Macquarie Street, the ground is embedded with a circular plaque dedicated to colonial architect Francis Greenway. It records all his principal designs: St Matthews at Windsor, Old Government House at Parramatta; Liverpool Hospital, Hobartville at Richmond, Macquarie Lighthouse at South Head, the Court House at Windsor, St Lukes at Liverpool, the Government Stables (today's Conservatorium of Music), Hyde Park Barracks, St James Church, and the Supreme Court. An impressive legacy for a former convict forger!

The coat of arms at the Supreme Court; the British lion and unicorn.

St James today, with the top of the Centrepoint tower above.

The gigantic Rum Hospital dominated Macquarie Street in the early 1800s

Part Two

The Elegance And Dramas Of Macquarie Street

12 Governor Lachlan Macquarie named **Macquarie Street** before us in one of his first acts in the colony. He was Australia's all-time champion at naming places after himself, his family, his mates and his superiors. During his governorship from 1810 to 1821, vain but able Macquarie, who held supreme power in the colony, so dubbed more than 150 places in New South Wales and (now) Tasmania.

Sydney's Elizabeth Street, for example, does not immortalise a queen. Macquarie named it after his wife, the former Elizabeth Campbell, along with Elizabeth and Campbell streets, streams and towns around the nation. He named places she liked to visit by the harbour Elizabeth Bay and Mrs Macquarie's Chair at Mrs Macquarie's Point. He made the names of streets in Old Sydney a *Who's Who* of Britain in the early 1800s.

Macquarie Street was the settlement's first grand avenue and is still, I believe, its most elegant. It became the aristocratic quarter in the mid 1800s, with scores of posh terrace townhouses flush with the footpath on its western side. To the east, the huge Sydney Hospital and other public buildings, the Botanic Gardens and The Domain.

Young ladies and gentlemen from other parts of town used to promenade in the street in their finery in the hope of impressing monied potential spouses. Despite the semi-tropical climate, the ladies wore mostly crinolines as they did in England; the gents were under chimney-pot hats with ties or fancy cravats and black cloth coats over waistcoats. On a quiet early morning it is still easy to imagine here the clatter of horses pulling hansom cabs. And the jolt of gangs of sullen convicts with Red Coat guards proceeding four abreast between the Barracks and their places of toil.

13 The northerly neighbour of the Barracks is the former **Australian Mint**, now the headquarters of the Historic Houses Trust of NSW and its public café, which is open on weekdays. The Trust is entrusted with the care of key historic buildings and sites in the State. Those on our Walk are the Hyde Park Barracks, Government House, the Museum of Sydney, the Justice and Police Museum and the Susannah Place Museum.

The Trust HQ is the nicely restored former south wing of the Rum Hospital (which we visit soon) and where sovereigns and half sovereigns were coined from gold won during a gold rush near Bathurst in the early 1850s. A sovereign was worth one pound, converting to $2 today, but a good weekly wage for many then.

The Trust's extensive Caroline Simpson Library & Research Collection is open to anyone interested in the history of house and garden design or interior furnishing. The Trust displays historical memorabilia here. A big courtyard excavated to reveal original stonework from the early 1800s connects with the Hyde Park Barracks. The building has an immense strong room where gold was stored after heavily-armed guards escorted it from the goldfields.

The little stone building between the old Mint and the wall of the barracks housed the soldiers who kept watch over the Mint's glistering ore. The building's façade includes 24 Georgian pane glass windows. It was the Australian branch of the Royal Mint from 1851 to 1901, then the Australian Mint for 26 years until minting was moved to Canberra when it became the national capital. The Historic Houses Trust is the preserver and saviour of many fine old places, and I thank you for doing such a magnificent job.

14 Next door is the **Sydney Hospital**, the working remainder of the grand establishment first dubbed the Rum Hospital. In the Australian vernacular, rum describes something that is queer, odd, strange. But the hospital's first name came from a seemingly dodgy deal done by

The Sydney Mint courtesy Historic Houses Trust of NSW photograph Deborah Ward

Governor Macquarie at no cost to the colonial coffers. The settlement sorely needed a decent public hospital as those at The Rocks and Parramatta were dilapidated and crowded. Short of cash, Macquarie in 1810 granted a group of entrepreneurs a three-year monopoly to import rum and spirits in return for building a massive hospital. The governor also provided 20 working convicts and 20 bullocks, along with their rations.

The developers were builder Garnham Blaxcell, Alexander Riley and Surgeon-General D'Arcy Wentworth. They imported 170,000 litres of Bengal rum and spirits for three shillings (30c.) a gallon duty and sold it to the grog-craved community for a whole lot more. The deal made them rich. And Sydney got a superb general hospital.

Superb architecturally, that is. In the early 1800s it cared for about 300 sick convicts. The wings north and south were barracks for apothecaries, surgeons and their staffs. The Rum Hospital as such was demolished and the present building opened in 1894.

A stone wall three metres high enclosed the complex to stop patients from escaping, we understand, as conditions at the hospital were harsh to the extent of being barbaric. Patients tried to supplement meager rations by cooking their own gruel amid the delirious cries of amputees and the insane.

As the privies were out in the yard, the corridors and the yard were usually full of patients with dysentery crawling on their knees to and from their wards. Wardsmen and 'nurses' were mostly convicts who were also locked up there at night. They stole patients' rations and humble belongings and had no sense of hygiene. A worthy matron here from 1852 to 1866 was picturesquely named Bathsheba Ghost. Proper nurses, urged upon the colony by an ageing Florence Nightingale, came later.

The presence of the hospital made the other side of Macquarie Street the domain of medical specialists to add to the street's elegant lustre. Societies of physicians and surgeons are still based here. An 1871 Victorian townhouse at 133 Macquarie is History House, the offices of the Royal Australian Historical Society. Architect George Allan Mansfield designed it as a residence for Parramatta pastoralist and politician George Oakes. For a while, this was home to the gentlemen's elite Reform Club, like the one in London's Pall Mall.

14

The rebuilt but stately shadow of the Old Rum Hospital, now Sydney Hospital.

15

Often in the shadows of modern high-rise blocks is a fountain honouring graduate nurses in the peaceful courtyard at Sydney Hospital.

15 Sydney Hospital's central block has endured. We recommend a visit to its courtyard off Macquarie Street. A fountain there is dedicated to the memory of the nurses who graduated from 1868 to 1985. It is a peaceful retreat from the city bustle; its colonial buildings loomed over by high-rise boxes to the west. The courtyard has an excellent café. From here you can stroll across quiet Kirkton Road to **The Domain**. Then, if you have the time, go over Art Gallery Road to the splendid Art Gallery of NSW.

The 40 hectares of The Domain have been preserved public open space since 1810. Its well-kept lawns and trees make it a popular lunch-time and jogging spot for office workers. There are regular social football, hockey and cricket matches. On Sunday afternoons, soap-box orators are given open go to expound their views to audiences of mostly hecklers. It's a fun spectacle. Soldiers gathered here before marching off to the Boer War and two world wars. The hungry and homeless who dossed down at The Domain in the 1930s Depression were fed at a soup kitchen north at Government House.

Cricket has been played here since the 1820s. In 1832, The Domain was the scene of the first cricket Test Match, between 'native youths' and 11 Englishmen. In an omen of what would face future 'Pommy' cricketers, the Aussies won.

Return through the hospital courtyard to Macquarie Street and continue north. Right here, a big wild boar of bronze by the footpath outside the hospital has long been a source of intrigue. It is *Il Porcellino,* a reproduction of a fountain in Florence. The Marchesa Fiaschi Torrigiani gave it to the people of Sydney in 1968 as a link in the friendship between Italy and Australia. It is a fundraiser for the hospital from people who are supposed to make a wish, toss in a coin and rub the boar's nose for good luck. Many have noticed, though, that the nose is not the only part of the pig that cops a rubbing for luck. Have a look at its shiny penis.

15

Wishers for luck, it seems, rub more than the nose of Macquarie Street's Il Percellino, a gift from Italy

Families enduring tough times during the Depression in 1931 pitched their tent homes at the Domain, with a soup kitchen nearby. Picture from The Sydney Morning Herald.

16 Behind its protective fence next door is **State Parliament House,** from where the State has been governed since 1829. It is the scene of many auspicious and dramatic moments, notably in the old days when statesmen and blockhead MPs stood toe to toe trading colourful invective. It was also once part of the Rum Hospital until some politicians moved in. The brick and stucco Legislative Council chamber, designed by Colonial Architect Mortimer Lewis, was added at the northern end in 1843.

Then another extension known as 'The Box' was added to the southern side. It is Sydney's only remaining building of prefabricated iron. The metal was shipped from England for a church for gold-rich Bendigo, Victoria, but the NSW Government bought it for £1,835 and had it lugged to Sydney. The building's gabled roof is a replacement of the original curved one. The front fence of iron bars with spiked tops is perhaps a necessary defence against regular groups of protesters and potential terrorists. The big figure of bronze keeping an eye on the Parliament from the southern side of the front courtyard is the ubiquitous Scot, Governor Macquarie.

The wide street going west from Macquarie Street to George Street is Martin Place. It is the hub of Sydney's financial district; home of the Reserve Bank of Australia. It is graced in the centre outside the General Post Office by the Cenotaph war memorial. Martin Place is marvellously wide today, unlike so many streets of Old Sydney that were formed for bullock and horse carts. It was widened in the wake of the 1890 Great Conflagration. Probably the worst fire ever in central Sydney, it raged through this area, gutting a lot of new and substantial buildings.

Keeping a beady eye on proceedings from the forecourt of the Parliament that kicked the Governor out of today's Government House (opposite), the venerable Governor Macquarie

17 By the trees bordering the **Mitchell Library** wing of the **State Library of NSW** is a big statue of the nation's great seafaring navigator, Captain Matthew Flinders, holding a sextant. He explored widely, often venturing to mountain tops to check his bearings. In a small sailboat with his shipmate surgeon George Bass, Flinders sailed around Tasmania to prove that it was an island. His maps of much of Australia's coast are still a primary reference. Mounted behind Flinders is a little statue of a cat! As the plaque here says, this is Trim, the navigator's spirited companion on voyages around much of the world. Flinders described Trim as, "The best and most illustrious of his race".

Around the corner to our right, near statues of a host of historical figures, mount the steps at the Greek columns to visit the magnificent Mitchell Library. It is the nation's outstanding hub of historical research publications and other references, and the source of many illustrations of Old Sydney in this book. The Mitchell houses the world's greatest collection of Australiana. The front doors of brass are etched with depictions dedicated to explorers of the Pacific. The floor of the lofty atrium has a magnificent copy in marble and brass of the map of New Holland, now Australia, by 1640s Dutch explorer Abel Tasman, credited with discovering Tasmania. The brass and marble illustration is the work of the Melocco brothers, who crafted the dazzling mosaic in the crypt of St Marys Cathedral. The Mitchell Library's huge main reading room, bordered by tiers of books, has a wonderful dominance of daylight, thanks to a big covering of glass under the roof with an automatic compensating battery of electric lights when the outside light fails. The imposing building of sandstone in the style of the Italian Renaissance was modified from a design by Government Architect Walter Vernon.

Reclusive collector David Scott Mitchell, a bachelor, in 1898 bequeathed much of his fantastic collection to the library. Not the Government, as he did not trust politicians. His 61,000 books, pictures and maps were the nucleus of today's collections. The pioneering Master of Arts from the University of Sydney also left a substantial fund for the collection's care and housing. His wealth came from his father, an army surgeon, whose farm north in the Hunter Valley had a rich seam of coal. David Mitchell was also patron of the

Sextant in hand, Captain Matthew Flinders, master navigator.

Australian Historical Society, later known as the Royal AHS.

His gift included original journals from James Cook and Joseph Banks, manuscripts from 17th century explorers Pedro de Quiros, his second in command de Torres, and Abel Tasman. Also the log of Captain (later NSW Governor) Bligh's mutiny ship *Bounty*. After receiving this lot, the Government of NSW squabbled and dallied for years over how and where to house it. Formidable Scot and book trade pioneer George Robertson (of Angus and Robertson

And by his master, a little statue of Flinders. cat Trim "...the most illustrious of his race".

bookstores) thundered at the legislative clots, demanding a home for "not only books but manuscripts, portraits, pictures, proclamations, broadsides, maps, medals ..." before American collectors began bidding for them. "Whenever I hear the money value of the Mitchell Collection spoken of," Robertson added, "I am tempted to break the peace." Building began on the first wing of the library in 1906, eight years after David Mitchell's gift. Nonetheless the library, added to over the years by other collectors including Sir William Dixson, another bachelor, is a priceless institution with about half a million publications that attracts scholars from around the world.

17

The grand Public Library of New South Wales, an architectural gem and Sydney's font of knowledge.

SNAPSHOT 1907
The amazing 'Old Four Hours'

PAUSE HERE to reflect on the life and death of an extraordinary man. He was a collector. Not just an ordinary collector, he was obsessed. Once this man spent ten hours in a shop, without food or drink, rummaging through the sale of another collector's collection. But then only a true collector can appreciate that hours disappear like minutes when engrossed in a hunt.

The euphoric sensations that sweep through a collector when unearthing a desirable item convert to utter contentment as a newly-acquired piece joins his collection. The pursuit for the next article, however, commences immediately.

David Scott Mitchell was such a collector, but he had something other collectors only dreamed of: wealth. His inheritance included rich coal-bearing land in the Hunter Valley, in northern NSW.

David used this wealth to amass the most amazing collection of Australiana. Books, manuscripts, pictures, engravings, maps, coins, tokens and medals. Some time around 1887 his desire for medieval manuscripts and early printed books of literature and poetry had turned wholly to collecting everything he could on Australia. He left no stone unturned. Every Monday morning a hansom cab conveyed David on his rounds of booksellers. For four hours he rummaged through the shelves and bargain bins looking for rare pieces.

These excursions were so regular that Sydney cabbies nicknamed him 'Old Four Hours'. David's reputation for buying Australiana became known internationally. People from around the world wrote to him offering rare items. Money was no object when it came to books but he had a different attitude about other things. We are told by a dealer that while selling him a parcel of manuscripts, a tradesman arrived to repair David's stove. David was infuriated that the workman wanted one pound 10 shillings ($3) for the work, but did not hesitate to pay £340 for the manuscripts. Once in 1906 he bought an entire collection of some 3,300 volumes just to obtain a few rare items it contained, particularly the hand-written *Endeavour* journals of Joseph (later Sir Joseph) Banks, for £5,700. The average yearly wage then was £103. By July of 1907 David Scott Mitchell was not a well man. He became bed-ridden but still received visitors bearing books. The late Fred Wymark, who worked for Angus and Robertson, arrived at David's bedside with a copy of Barron Field's *First Fruits of Australian Poetry*, the first book of poetry printed in Australia. David was elated and said, "I did not think I would ever see this. I have been looking for it for years." With that, David gave a gasp and fell back on his pillow. Fred was turning to leave and report David's death when he was startled to hear, "Well, where were we, Fred?"

David Mitchell died a few days later, on 24 July 1907, of pernicious anaemia. He was buried at Rookwood Cemetery beside his parents' graves. Through an oversight or neglect, no inscription to David was carved on his parents' existing headstone.

This was not rectified until 24 July 1987, when a small group of people stood in drizzling rain to unveil the new inscription and commemorate a patriotic Australian who gave us the nucleus of our rich and incomparable, documented history.

...dney in 1919 welcoming home soldiers from World War I as they parade past the then-new Mitchell ...brary building. Mitchell Library, State Library of NSW.

18 We suggest a saunter north from the library, east of Macquarie Street, through the **Royal Botanic Gardens**. In a strip in the road we cross is a magnificent collection of bronze images of William Shakespeare and characters from his plays. Also near here is a brass relief honouring the steeds of the Australia's heroic Light Horse Brigade of World War I. In colonial times, the brigade's brick barracks stood where the library is now. The splendid gardens, marvellously endowed with old Moreton Bay fig trees, are on the site of the colony's original farm, which eventually failed. The first furrows were ploughed here in 1788, with grazing sheep, horses, cattle, goats and pigs astounding the local Aborigines.

A short walk north takes us to Achille Simonetti's grandiose High Victorian fountain featuring a misleadingly-pompous statue of long-nosed little Arthur Phillip, the colony's first governor, looking to Sydney Heads and holding a scroll. A furled flag is at his side.

The modest, non-nonsense administrator would have blushed at this representation of him among little water spouts from the cheeks of sea monsters and, inexplicably beyond understanding, sculptures of the mythical gods Cyclops and Neptune. The sides of the fountain also feature tributes to Agriculture and Commerce, along with bronze plaques of Aborigines and the bows of four sailing ships heading north, south, east and west. Phillip's statue was cast in Florence and erected for the celebrations of the Jubilee of Queen Victoria's reign.

Phillip, incidentally, was revered by indigenous Cadigal clan members who watched from bushes as soon as the leader of the First Fleet stepped ashore, and smiled. Because a front tooth was missing! The Cadigals had a tradition of knocking out a front tooth as an initiation into manhood. We suppose they reckoned Phillip of the missing chopper, in his fancy clothes of authority, was illustrating a commanding kinship with them. Tickled pink, the governor wrote home to London about it: "On my showing them that I wanted a front tooth it occasioned a general clamour, and I thought gave me some little merit in their opinion". And (generally) he treated the Aborigines with respect, as directed by King George III.

Sydney's grand Garden Palace of timber stood at the site of Phillip's fountain.

*William Shakespeare, keeping an eye
on the State Library.*

*Superbly-carved characters from the
master's plays.*

18

Neptune's fork challenging a leaden sky beside the grandiose depiction of Governor Arthur Phillip in the Botanic Gardens.

The palace was built for Australia's first International Exhibition in 1879, then used as an occasional concert hall and archives store until fire razed it in 1882, with the loss of precious records.

The Botanic Gardens sweep from near the Opera House, around Farm Cove to Woolloomooloo Bay. You might wonder how Woolloomooloo, the suburb east of here, got its strange name. There are lots of (often crazy) notions, but the hot favourite is that it is a corruption by white pioneers of the Aboriginal name for a young kangaroo, Wullallmullah.

We recommend the garden's spring walk through seasonal flowers, seeing specimens of nearly every Australian orchid variety at the orchid house, a botanical delight in the herbarium, and a vale of tropical rainforest studded with a huge range of palms, called 'the palmery'. It is a magnificent reserve in the heart of the city, with duck and fish ponds, the achievement of 220 years of thoughtful plantings and cultivation with eyes to scientific research, leisure and beauty.

The real Governor Phillip (1738-1814)

19 Continue north from the Arthur Phillip Fountain and leave the Botanic Gardens through the Palace Gardens Gate at Macquarie Street. Just north is the big, white fairytale-like **Conservatorium of Music**, with battlements on the walls and widely known as 'The Con'. It was originally built as a horse stable!

Convict architect Francis Greenway, to whom Governor Macquarie gave a pardon for his works, designed the building to house the Governor's horses and also some servants. With respect to Greenway, why all those battlements? To protect the horses from organised attack?

The lavish grandness of the castellated 'horse house' so outraged the good folk of the near-bankrupt colony and a grump of an imperial inspector from London in 1819 that Greenway's plans for a much-grander vice-regal residence nearby were scrapped. Surely this was the most elaborate stable on earth. Although folk and some classical music wafted around the colonial settlement from rare concerts, bawdy ballads generally came from fiddlers, pianists and singers in taverns, plus hungry street buskers and minstrels.

For its first 125 years, Old Sydney had no real musical heart. Hot campaigning by music lovers resulted in the State Government founding the Conservatorium, a Chair of Music and a symphony orchestra as Australians left their new nation by the shipload in 1914 to fight for Britain in World War I. The governor's horses were moved out and the inaugural concert was held here a year later. The Con, home of the University of Sydney Music and a centre of research and learning, is the heart of the nation's classical music today.

The Conservatorium of Music, originally built to stable Governor Macquarie's horses. And battlements to defend them from attack?

20

The newly-built Government House presided grandly by Farm Cove, c. 1845. Mitchell Library, State Library of NSW.

20 A rewarding diversionary stroll, if you have an extra hour or so, begins through the old gates to the road and path in the vast gardens immediately north of 'The Con' towards Bennelong Point. We pass mature trees and shrubs for half a kilometre to reach imperious Government House. No longer the private residence of the NSW Governor of the day, it is still the Governor's official residence, and the building and grounds are usually open to the public in daytime. Free guided tours are from 10.30am to 3pm Fridays to Sundays, however it's advised you check as Government House is occasionally closed to the public for vice-regal events and functions.

The towered, turreted and crenellated Gothic Revival mansion with heraldic stone carvings is Sydney's third Government House, if one counts Arthur Phillip's canvas prefabricated one and the residence built next to it in Bridge Street, where we will be soon. Its design was sent from London in 1836 by a young Queen Victoria's very own Royal Architect, Edward Blore, who never saw the site. Blore designed extensions to Buckingham Palace and tarted up Hampton Court and Windsor Castle with prissy adornments so typical of Victorian buildings and statuary we see in Sydney.

Construction of Government House from stone quarried at suburban Pyrmont, with staircasing of red cedar from the Shoalhaven and Hunter valleys, and chimney pieces of local marble, began in 1837. James Barnet's grand entrance portico was added in 1874.

Australia's first Governor-General, the Earl of Hopetoun, moved in here after Federation in 1901. The NSW Governor returned 14 years later. Then in the late 1900s a State Labor Government unceremoniously banished its Governor, officially its boss and the representative of the Queen of England and Australia, from his traditional home. An unprecedented act, but at least it opened Government House to general public tours and ceremonial events.

Part Three

Sydney and Police Museums,
Ground Zero, Opera House

AHEAD IS a short stroll through the historical heart of Sydney. We visit the site of the arrival of the First Fleet, the first Government House and Circular Quay, the stamen from which a nation flowered. And Sydney's little-known Ground Zero!

If you went to Government House, return to Macquarie Street and cross it by the Conservatorium to enter still-gracious old Bridge Street. Overwhelming the intersection is the gigantic bronze statue of a regal-looking fellow on a horse. The subject is King Edward VII, who reigned for 10 years from Australia's Federation year, 1901. The flamboyant and wayward monarch with several mistresses was crowned after the death of his mother, Queen Victoria. Bridge Street was named so because a footbridge further down here, the settlement's first bridge, crossed the sweet and gladed rivulet that was later named the Tank Stream.

21 The sturdy building of Pyrmont sandstone on the southwest corner, extending powerfully on four floors along Bridge Street to Phillip Street, sternly facing off a similar shadow of itself across the street, is the headquarters of the State Chief Secretary's Department, originally a political powerhouse as the **Colonial Secretary's Office**. Colonial Secretaries such as Sir Henry Parkes wielded enormous influence, pretty well in charge of the nuts and bolts of government, from elegant rooms here with paneling of Borneo cedar.

The statues over the building's Macquarie Street corner exemplifying Mercy, Justice and Wisdom are by Giovanni Fontana. Take a look in the impressive entrance foyer, which has information plaques about the past of this Italian Renaissance triumph by Colonial architect James Barnet in 1878. Also there is a statue of the Maid of NSW with a sheep and a horn of plenty.

The former Colonial Secretary's Office, a defiant bastion from colonial governance at the corner of Macquarie and Bridge Streets.

21

22 Mercifully saved from the wreckers is a row of three-level Georgian terraces with verandahs just up Phillip Street, which we cross to come to a highlight of our Walk, **The Museum of Sydney.** With its excellent book and gift shop and café, the museum holds an entertaining, fascinating record of Old Sydney. A feature your author likes is a display of detailed models of the 11 ships of the First Fleet.

This is the site of the colony's first governors' residences, with sentry boxes in the front courtyard. A garden sloped gently from here to the shore of Sydney Cove, less than 20 metres away. Governors had clear views from the residence of their domain, including The Rocks and down the harbour to the Sydney Heads. The first government house here was the canvas prefabricated version Arthur Phillip shipped from England. A Georgian residence of six rooms replaced it in 1789. It was Sydney's first two-storey house, the first with glass windows, a staircase and the first using fired bricks. After 56 years, a worthy structure of stone went up. It became a leaky place, attacked by white ants and dry rot, the bane of the colony's early governors. They were nagged a lot by their wives until the completion of the grand new Government House by Bennelong Point in 1845 and the old one was demolished. Sick and ineffectual Governor Sir George Gipps was the last of nine colonial bosses to live in Bridge Street, where the first meeting of the NSW Legislative Assembly was held 1824. Archeological digs in recent years have revealed the stone footings of the first real Government House. You can see them through glass from an innovative display in front of the museum.

This was where soldiers of the corrupt Rum Corps enacted the nation's sole military insurrection, the Rum Rebellion, by arresting and supplanting Governor William Bligh on the hot night 26 January 1808. It was the 20th anniversary of the founding of the colony, now the date of Australia Day. Bligh had been the captain of the British Navy's *Bounty* whose crew mutinied in the Pacific in 1789. He and 18 loyal crew members were left at the mercy of the ocean, crammed into an open launch which was only seven metres long. In one of the world's great feats of navigation, and sometimes pursued by cannibals, William Bligh sailed the launch for 47 days of deprivation 6,710 km to safety in Timor.

Bligh was arrested at the behest of powerful and corrupt graziers including John Macarthur because he supported the small farmers the greedy rich

Reigning with his reins, King Edward VII, monarch for 10 years after Australia's Federation, at the junction of Macquarie and Bridge Streets.

Convict artist John Eyre's stylised painting of Government House, circa 1807. Mitchell Library, State Library of NSW.

According to artist G.E. Peacock, camels grazed in the Government House gardens, now occupied by Bridge Street, in 1845. Dixson Galleries, State Library of NSW.

pastoralists were exploiting, and because he had the fortitude to try to break the military officers' monopoly of trade, notably in rum. This gave them a strangle-hold on the colony's economy, as rum was the major currency. Sydney virtually ran out of cash soon after white settlement, as all money was minted and printed in England. Most of the cash the pioneer settlers brought here soon went off to England and India to buy materials, food and grog. Very little cash came back to the colony as there were few exports.

Rum Corps Major George Johnston became the colony's administrator for six months. William Bligh was kept under house arrest in Government House and its garden for 14 months. Governor Macquarie arrived in 1810 with his own regiment and disbanded the Rum Corps. Johnston was eventually found guilty of mutiny at trial in London but he returned to the colony in 1811 as a free settler. And he did nicely. He acquired Annandale Farm, dubbed after Johnston's home patch in Scotland, and now the suburb of that name.

SNAPSHOT 1808
Here Comes The Band ... And Rebellion

HAVE YOU EVER stood in a particular place and wished you could slip back in time, to see what it was really like? For me it's at the corner of Pitt and Bridge Streets. To stand on the first, sandstone bridge spanning the old Tank Stream, the life-blood of the infant colony, and watch the passing parade. Merchants astride their mounts and genteel couples in horse-drawn gigs bestowing nods of recognition as they pass familiar faces.

Watching thirsty sailors striding out towards The Rocks and the many taverns there. A few clusters of NSW Corps soldiers are discussing the problems of the colony and giving disdainful glances to neatly-attired emancipists as they saunter by. Bullock teams with heavy loads lumber over the makeshift dirt roads full of ruts and potholes. The occasional gang of convicts shuffles past.

Imagine you are standing on that little bridge around 6.30 on the hot evening of 26 January 1808. As an advance party of four officers of the NSW Corps turns into Bridge Street from High Street (now George) we hear in the distance the beating of drums. Next to turn into Bridge Street is Major George Johnston with other officers of the Corps. Are they celebrating this colony's 20th anniversary? No.

The beating of the drums becomes louder and we hear the fifes. As the ranks of soldiers wheel into Bridge Street, with colours flying, you realise there are hundreds of red jackets with white leather cross-straps, shiny boots, gleaming brass insignias on the soldiers' shakos. Muskets are held firmly over their shoulders, fixed bayonets.

They march with determination, as they have one objective – to overthrow the Governor. They continue advancing to the gates of Government House. The advance parties are met at the gates by a dainty but fiery Mary Putland, the daughter of Governor William Bligh. She has in hand a parasol, which she flays into every armed soldier who comes within striking distance. Her distress is evident to all. "You traitors!" she cries. "You rebels." Mary, whose husband has died but two weeks back, pleads with the soldiers to take her life in place of her father's. Several soldiers gain entry into Government House and search for Bligh. They find him upstairs, hiding official papers, not hiding under the bed as the later political cartoon will portray. Johnston places Bligh under house arrest and we now have a new, but acting, Governor of NSW ... for the time being.

23 Continue down Bridge Street from the museum, over Young and Loftus Streets. Then cross Bridge Street to the very hub of Sydney, the little triangular park with Moreton bay fig trees called **Macquarie Place**. This traditional site of Aboriginal corroborees now has two cardinal national relics of white settlement.

Once Government House's vegetable garden, surrounded by an orchard and cottages, Governor Macquarie intended it to be the core of administrative Sydney. He had life-sentence convict Edward Cureton lead a team in 1818 to build a modest fingerpost of an obelisk here to mark the spot as such. The marker's original plaque, designed by Francis Greenway, still clearly says it is: 'To record that all the public roads leading to the interior of the Colony are measured from it. L. Macquarie Esq., Governor.' It is still, but the little-known, Ground Zero of Sydney, from where road distances are measured. The convict-hewn marker is beside Loftus Street.

Macquarie the visionary, a stickler for correctness, must have had a good reason to plant his marker right here. And there is evidence from the 1800s that it was here, not at other officially and unofficially declared locations, that the nation's first flagstaff was raised, claiming the land for England. Your author reckon this is so, but the matter will continue to be debated.

Macquarie Place's other noted relic, near the centre of the triangle, is a huge anchor or iron that once held HMS *Sirius*, the ship named after the southern sky's brightest star and the lead ship of the First Fleet. The anchor is a rare actual souvenir from the First Fleet, despite being submerged at Norfolk Island for 117 years after *Sirius* was wrecked there. Divers finally recovered the anchor in 1907.

The enormous bronze statue on the Bridge Street side of Macquarie Place is of a colossus of industry, Thomas Sutcliffe Mort (1816 – 1878). He was a pioneer of Australia's wool exporting industry, a founder of the AMP Society and a generous contributor to social welfare. Mort's Dock and Bay at Balmain, where he had vast wool stores (as well as at Circular Quay), are named after him. Mort's statue has been there since 1883.

The waterway that trickled over a little beach of sand at Sydney Cove, the 'run of clear water' that enticed our first settlers, still runs north under Bridge

PRINCIPAL ROADS.
DISTANCE FROM SYDNEY
TO BATHURST   137 M
FROM SYDNEY TO WINDSOR 35 D
TO PARRAMATTA 15
TO LIVERPOOL   20
TO MACQUARIE TOWER

Ground Zero. Governor Macquarie's modest obelisk in Macquarie Place marking the spot from where all road travel in the colony was measured. It is still the cartographic hub of NSW.

Street and everything else some 50 metres west of here, near today's Pitt Street. Governor Phillip had pits dug in the stream's sandstone base to become water stores during dry weather in the colony's infancy. Virtual water storage tanks, they were, so Phillip called the waterway the Tank Stream. The stream's valley teemed with kangaroos, possums, koalas and more than 50 types of birds. It was lush with ferns, Sydney red gums, myrtles and golden flowering mimosas. These were soon better known as wattles, an emblem of Australia and the origin of the gold in the nation's sporting colours. The new name came after mimosas were cut down and used to construct huts of wattle-and-daub walls (wattle rods being interwoven with mud or clay as reinforcing).

Back in Loftus Street, go north past little Reiby Place, named after teenage convict Mary Reibey, which some spell without the second 'e' and was pronounced 'Rabey'. Mary (nee Haycock) lived here. She bore seven children, became Australia's richest woman and is pictured on the Australian $20 note.

24 Fittingly, just past Reiby Place is a remarkable little public reserve at the former site of the colony's first stores building, erected in 1792 and for 20 years the hub of commerce and trade. The reserve opposite the Gallipoli Club is now the **Jesse Street Gardens**, in memory of social justice and women's rights campaigner Jesse (1889–1970) and honouring the indomitable, brave, gallant, canny and generous women who so importantly moulded this nation. Thanks for it go to the Fellowship of First Fleeters and the Women's Pioneer Society.

An array of sculptures and plaques in the reserve honour Aboriginal women, convicts, defence personnel in several wars, emancipists and working mothers during the hard times of Old Sydney. Queen Victoria is the only woman we have seen immortalised by statuary elsewhere in the city.

After 117 years underwater with the wreck of HMS Sirius, *her anchor was salvaged as a rare relic from the First Fleet at Macquarie Place.*

The vital role of women in the growth of the nation is recognised by statuary in Jesse Street Park in Loftus Street representing motherhood and families and also women at war.

A WALK IN OLD SYDNEY

25 Cross Loftus Street to a Union Flag of Queen Anne on a staff of metal planted in the footpath. The British lost the American War of Independence under this flag. The cross of St Patrick, representing Ireland, came later to complete the Union Jack. This modest presentation is what your author deduces to be the officially-declared site on 26 January 1788 of the **first raising of the flag** of Britain in Sydney. A plaque here says so. It also says the location was determined in 1963 by a committee including the Lord Mayor, the Chief Justice of the Supreme Court, the Surveyor-General and the Director of Parks. Today's flag was raised on Australia Day in 1976.

It is strange that no colonial governor glorified this spot. In 1788, high tide in Sydney Cove would have at least reached here. We prefer to think Governor Macquarie knew where the flag was first raised to claim this continent in the name of his monarch and placed his obelisk there in 1818. We refer, of course, to the Ground Zero marker just up and across Loftus Street. Others reckon the location was at The Rocks. Good grist, it is, for history buffs.

The Paragon Hotel, at the end of Loftus Street, is one of Sydney's most colourful public houses, well worth a visit. And around the corner to the left, where Alfred Street meets Pitt Street, is the Ship Inn, a now-gracious favourite of old salts and young for generations. Another distinctive establishment in this area heavily-endowed with heritage hotels is The Republic, just up Pitt Street. Dwarfed today by plush new establishments, The Republic opened in 1865 as the Exchange Hotel, being then near the Royal Stock Exchange. It was rebuilt in 1880.

25

The Republic Hotel opened in 1865.

26

The flagstaff is beside the western wall of Sydney's celebrated old **Customs House**, which we should enter just around the corner off Alfred Street, named of course after Queen Victoria's consort. Many people get a shock when they enter the building to see, imbedded in the floor of the foyer, a host of what look like black Nazi swastikas!

But Hitler's symbol, logo if you like, has clockwise arms, the reverse of these ancient signs. His was the female version! The swastika dates back to prehistoric times in Africa, Europe and India to symbolize virility, wealth, good fortune. The Customs House's swastikas have been there since the early 1900s, predating the Nazi Party. Also in the floor, and under glass that we can walk over, is an amazing scale model of Sydney.

Robert Paton's Lion and Unicorn royal coat of arms over the building's portico is among the best stone carvings in Australia. The clock face intertwining a trident and dolphin was added in 1887.

An array of these in the floor often startle visitors in the Customs House foyer. But they were installed long before the Nazi swastika, which is the reverse, or female, version of this ancient symbol of good fortune.

The Customs House, a colonial survivor at Circular Quay.

The Customs House stands like a lone survivor of Sydney's Victorian commercial buildings, mostly colourful taverns, among today's high-rise concrete and glass towers at the city's maritime gateway.

It was the city's third customs house, the vital checker and collector of duty payments on imports, built in 1885. Customs collections were a major source of income for the government in Old Sydney. A two-floor Georgian Customs House built in 1844 was demolished. The building's fourth floor was added in 1900. A fifth floor and attic came 17 years later and an interior courtyard was roofed to provide more office space.

East along Alfred Street is the tall, curve-fronted AMP Centre, where Thomas Mort's grand brick and stone wool store of five floors stood for more than 100 years. The marvellous painter of colonial Australia, Conrad Martens, who came to the colony in 1835, had a studio in there. Perhaps Mort, long dead, would not have minded the demolition of his store in 1960 for the AMP Centre to be built as he was a founder of the AMP Society of insurers. Your author remembers the excitement in Sydney in 1962 about the erection of the AMP Centre, the city's first skyscraper, an amazing 117 metres high.

27 Further east, at the corner of Alfred and Phillip Streets, is the 1853 **Justice and Police Museum**. Open only at weekends, this former Water Police Court and Police Station of sandstone holds a remarkable record, with lots of souvenirs, models and photographs of the seedy and crooked sides of Old Sydney. The criminal courts are there just as when felons were tried in the 1800s. It also had a couple of windowless prison cells likened at the time to the Black Hole of Calcutta.

Items displayed include weapons presented in evidence, against even notorious bushrangers: coshes, knuckle-dusters, handcuffs, hatchets and scores of deadly-looking knives and hand guns, shot guns and rifles. The building's classic revival design by Edmund Blacket and its weathered sandstone make it look older than its 155 years.

The Water Police today deal with matters only on the water. But in seafaring colonial Sydney, the Water Police would have a go at just about anything, including traffic law violations. In December 1880, the Water Police Court dealt with bounders for 'driving (horsedrawn coaches, I assume) across the intersections of streets at a pace faster than a walk'. The guilty had to pay costs plus fines of up to 10 shillings, about a week's wages then.

The Water Police Court also dished out harsh punishment to two enterprising gents who presented at premises in Pitt Street in November 1880 an exhibition portraying the bushranger Ned Kelly, recently-hanged in Melbourne, as a hero. *The Sydney Morning Herald* reported that the stars of the show were Ned's sister Kate Kelly, his brother James and dead Ned's grey mare Kitty. The court was told the crowd paying a shilling (10c.) each to see them included 'boys from 12 to 20 years of age, girls of the larrikin and disorderly classes' and that constables had to keep order on the footpath outside. A police officer testified that he considered the exhibition of Kate riding a horse, and a sort of reenactment of some of Ned's life, 'a gross outrage, and highly injurious to public morals'. The court closed down the show.

From the museum, cross Alfred Street, go north under the Cahill Expressway and railway line to the eastern side of Circular Quay, past a wall of glassy, high-rise apartments at our right that replaced sandstone wool stores and warehouses, towards Bennelong Point.

Weary and unwashed passengers and crew on the First Fleet of ships anchored in the Cove, waiting anxiously to go ashore, waiting for a week in some instances, saw here a long spit like a burred spear piercing the Harbour. Much of it was covered by a huge midden of sun-bleached shells from oysters, scallops and mussels up to 10 metres deep, evidence of thousands of years of feasting on the bountiful shore by Aborigines. It was first called Cattle Point as a bull, a bull calf and four cows delivered on the First Fleet were pastured on the tidal island here. Later, this shore was often crammed with windjammers. A walkway along here is called the Tarpeian Way, after the point's Tarpeian Rock which projected like the spine of a dinosaur, reminding some pioneers of the rock in ancient Rome from which traitors were tossed to their deaths. The rock was quarried in 1817 for building blocks.

Bennelong Point is named after a native man of the Gayimai (Manly) tribe whom Governor Phillip ordered to be kidnapped in front of his wailing kin in 1789. Another young man stolen at the time, Colby, escaped from Government

The former Water Police court and station, now the Justice and Police Museum, packed with tools and tales of crime in Old Sydney.

Circular Quay had become a busy place of commerce by 1892. The massive building on the left (where the AMP building is today) was Mort's Wool store. To its right, the first Customs House. Mitchell Library, State Library of NSW.

27

House after gnawing through the rope attached to his leg irons. A scrubbed Bennelong, however, in his mid 20s, soon adopted European ways and food, brandy and wine before leaping a fence and running away to his family.

Phillip found Bennelong with some 200 other Aborigines feasting on a dead stranded whale at Manly. In an act now thought to have been orchestrated by Bennelong in retribution for his abduction, one of the tribe speared the Governor in the shoulder before the whites escaped in their longboats. Bennelong, however, having tasted the pleasures of white civilization, returned

Breakers of the colony's harsh laws were tried at the Water Police Court after being charged around the corner (right) at the Water Police Station at the Circular Quay end of Phillip Street. The buildings were in their prime here from 1856. Mitchell Library, State Library of NSW.

to the Governor's table in 1790. The native remained, virtually a noble mascot and servant in the court of the Governor. Dressed in a ruffled shirt and breeches, Bennelong accompanied Phillip in 1792 when the Governor returned to England. The Aborigine became a novelty of society and was presented to King George III. He returned to Sydney with the new Governor Hunter in 1795. Bennelong remained an unhappy misfit, not accepted by his fellow tribe or whites. He died after a tribal fight in 1813 and was buried at Kissing Point, Ryde.

28 We are, of course, heading for the **Sydney Opera House**, the landmark wonder of architecture with a roof depicting spinnaker sails of yachts that have worked and played on Sydney Harbour since the First Fleet. This hub of the nation's operatic and concert activities and the Harbour Bridge are the most photographed structures in the city. The then-high cost was covered largely by a series of Opera House lotteries.

The building is just as impressive on the inside, with fine acoustics in its theatres. It was built amid controversy about its bold style and the cost after its Danish architect Joern Utzon won a design competition against 221 other submissions. Verbal assaults on him during construction caused Utzon to resign from the project in 1966 but the building was completed by Australian architects to his design in 1973. A trip he made to Mexico inspired the design of the massive stone base and terraced stairways, like the Aztec and Mayan temples he visited. Queen Elizabeth opened the Opera House in 1975.

28

Sydney Opera House. Renovation work including a tunnel for deliveries and stage sets is scheduled to start in early 2011 and finish by 2013.

Part Four

Sydney Cove, Suez Canal, The Rocks Visitor Centre

AHEAD IS the heart of the early days of Sydney, rich in tales of heroism and horrors. We see perhaps its oldest building, an ancient well and learn how The Rocks was saved from destruction. A fortune from a bank robbery may be buried around here.

29 Stroll to the busy ferry wharves at **Circular Quay**, a popular beat for some engaging buskers, following the NSW government's Writers Walk, which over the next few hundred metres around the waterfront has embedded at our feet plaques honouring many of Australia's authors and foreign authors who wrote about Sydney.

Among them is celebrated Polish author and sailor of the world, Joseph Conrad, who spent a lot of time in Australia. In *Mirror of the Sea*, Conrad in 1906 described the Quay as "the integral part of the finest, most beautiful, vast, and safe bay the sun has ever shone upon".

Sydney Cove has had some historic moments. The Second Fleet of 'hell ships' arrived here in 1790 with 1,006 convicts after a terrible voyage in awful conditions during which 267 died. A further 486 of them arrived seriously ill. The Third Fleet came a year later, with more convicts, including the first prisoners directly from Ireland. The first ferry service to the North Shore began by 1811, run by a former convict, the West Indian Billy Blue.

Colonials were intrigued to see ships making speedy way on the harbour against the wind and even when there was no wind. Curiosity turned to fear for the sailors when they realised the ships were driven from fires in their bellies that belched smoke through chimneys. *Sophia Jane* in 1831 was the first steamship to travel to Australia and operated up and down the coast until 1845. Steamships were built in Darling Harbour from 1836.

Amid patriotic pomp and tears in 1855, a regiment of young Australians marched through the city and sailed off to fight for the Queen in the Crimea War in the Sudan. *The Sydney Morning Herald* commented at the time that

Chusan, an early steamship in Sydney in 1852, powered from a fire in her belly and a chimney coughing smoke, rated a special music sheet.

Now you know why it is called Circular Quay. More accurately, it was perhaps jokingly in 1844, Semi-circular Quay, created by convicts who toiled in slime to reclaim several hectares of mud flats by the mouth of the Tank Stream. Illustrated Sydney News. Mitchell Library, State Library of NSW.

the troops' departure "put forth [the colony's] claims to be recognised as an integral part of the British Empire". The same day, the paper lamented that the head of the British army in the Sudan, General Gordon, had just been killed. Australians also joined the American Civil War in the 1860s.

Hundreds of convicts marched down from the Hyde Park Barracks and toiled for more than a year in slime to reclaim about four hectares of tidal flats below the government gardens. They finished the job, the settlement's last big convict-worked enterprise, in 1844.

Thousands of citizens rioted violently in 1888 to try to stop two shiploads of Chinese from landing in Sydney. One lot of about 60 Chinese, on *Afghan*, had been turned away from Melbourne. *Tsinan* arrived with 204 Chinese immigrants, but only some of them were destined for Sydney. The number is still debated, but at least 50 industrious immigrants landed safely under police protection to become significant contributors to the city's growth. The rioters blamed the Chinese for an outbreak of smallpox in 1881 as the first victim was a Chinese lad. State Parliament even passed a Chinese Restriction Act.

Many find it odd that the rectangular cove is called Circular Quay. It was never circular. But in 1837 an act was passed by the NSW Government for the construction of 'Circular Quay'. It was never intended to be called anything else. The plans show it to be more like three quarters of a circle. In the mid-1840s it was half finished when an economic depression hit and work stopped. Plans from then calling it 'Semi-circular Quay' could have been the work of a departmental joker. The Quay was finished to plan by 1860.

The Tank Stream was gradually channeled, then covered by buildings. Work in the 1890s and the 1940s straightened the arc of Circular Quay and finger-jetties were built for the city's growing fleet of commuter and sightseeing ferries. Venice has its gondolas; Sydney its ferries.

When white settlers arrived, a grand swamp oak tree presided near where George Street meets the Quay. It survived until a gang of street repairers thoughtlessly cut it down in 1832. *The Sydney Morning Herald* at the time said the first settlers flew their flag from the oak to claim this land for England and that Governor Macquarie revered the tree. Some historians swear that this spot, not by today's Loftus Street, is where that first flag fluttered.

Buried Treasure!

PERHAPS BURIED around here is a fortune in old money, the proceeds of the nation's first bank robbery. Just south of the Quay up George Street was the Bank of Australia, from where £14,000, worth $6 billion by today's values, was cleverly stolen in 1828. The loot, it seems, remains buried not far from the bank. Hundreds of hopeful diggers, working mostly in the night so they would not have to declare their find, seem to have failed to find it.

Wealthy landowners, contemptuous of the new Bank of New South Wales, opened the bank next to a pub owned by the colony's former chief constable, John Redman. Bricklayer Tom Turner, who had helped build the Bank of Australia in the first place and also a drain beside it, knew a big drain ran under the bank to the Tank Stream, nearby to the east. He revealed this to some criminal mates and recommended the robbery.

Those mates were former convict James Dingle, highway robber Will Blackstone and a 'fence' (receiver of stolen goods) Tom Woodward. No doubt on a promise for a slice of the action, Turner did not take part. He reckoned that because of his inside knowledge he would be a quick and prime suspect. The gang spent a couple of weekends, sustained by rum, hacking away at the wall of the dark, dank and putrid drain. With a nice piece of calculation, they broke through to the bank's strong room and took off with the money in notes, Spanish dollars and Georgian silver coins. Perhaps in their haste, they left behind a box containing £2,000 worth of gold sovereigns.

The banker victims were generally detested and the highly-publicised robbery was greeted with applause in the lawless community. The robbers would have got away with it, but Blackstone 'grassed'. An habitual criminal who committed another highway robbery, Blackstone turned them in years after the bank heist. His reward was a pardon but he was in and out of jail until his death in 1850. The robbers and Turner were jailed, never, the story goes, to reveal the location of their booty. However, about a year after the robbery a publican named Boreham, of a pub at The Rocks, was jailed on Norfolk Island for knowingly receiving money, proceeds of a robbery at the Bank of Australia. Regardless, the bankers never got their money back.

The Rocks Map

THE ROCKS, with its rough, tough but heroic beginnings, surely rivals anywhere in Australia for colourful heritage. We want you to soak up the present and past of this scene of Sydney's raw beginnings, its first shanty town roistered by gangs of larrikins, crammed now with a mix of smart restaurants, shops, houses and hotels … and surviving 1800s relics, pubs, stores, shady lanes and convict-cut cliffs where some humble terrace homes nestle. Your author has spent a long time planning the best circuit stroll of The Rocks, marked on our large-scale map opposite, so you see nearly all of it.

FROM THE WHARVES at the Quay, continue by the waterfront past First Fleet Park, nicely studded with trees and probably hosting pigeons, ducks, magpies, mynas, sparrows, ibis and parrots on our left. In front of the vast Museum of Contemporary Art, the former home of the Maritime Services Board, is a small, bronze bust that is evidently a faithful likeness of Governor Arthur Phillip, unveiled in 1954. Phillip, by the way, was reluctant to despatch felons to the gallows. He said he would rather set murderers loose in New Zealand, where Maoris would eat them. Continue north across the base of Argyle Street to a park where a life-size statue of a seafarer on a pedestal germanely surveys the traffic on Sydney Cove.

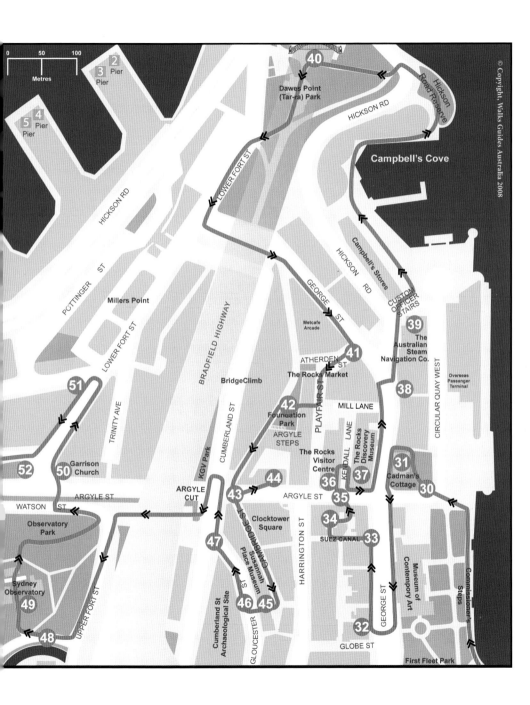

© Copyright, Walks Guides Australia 2008

0   50   100
Metres

40
Dawes Point
(Tar-ra) Park
HICKSON RD

Campbell's Cove

HICKSON RD

2 Pier
3 Pier
4 Pier
5 Pier

Campbell's Stores

HICKSON   RD

CUSTOM OFFICER STAIRS

POTTINGER   ST
Millers Point

LOWER FORT ST

HICKSON RD

LOWER FORT ST

GEORGE   ST

Metcafe
Arcade

39
The
Australian
Steam
Navigation Co.

Overseas
Passenger
Terminal

CIRCULAR QUAY WEST

51
BRADFIELD HIGHWAY

BridgeClimb

41
ATHERDEN ST
The Rocks Market

42
Foundation
Park
ARGYLE
STEPS

PLAYFAIR ST

MILL LANE

38

The Rocks
Discovery
Museum

KENDALL LANE

TRINITY AVE

CUMBERLAND ST

KGV Park

The Rocks
Visitor
Centre

31
Cadman's
Cottage

52   **50**
Garrison
Church

ARGYLE
CUT

43

44

36   **37**

35

30

ARGYLE ST

WATSON   ST

ARGYLE ST

HARRINGTON ST

GEORGE ST

Museum of
Contempory Art

Commissioners Steps

Observatory
Park

Clocktower
Square

34

SUEZ CANAL

33

47

Susannah
Place Museum

GLOUCESTER ST

Sydney
Observatory
49

Cumberland St
Archaeological Site

46   **45**

GLOUCESTER ST

UPPER FORT ST

48

32

GLOBE ST

First Fleet Park

30 This chap with the nautical air and hat of authority is Captain William Bligh, master navigator, later Governor of the colony and victim of the *Bounty* mutiny and the Rum Rebellion reported on in Part 3. Note the scar on Bligh's left cheek. No, it was not from a fight with the mutineers. The scar was his legacy from a day in England when young Will was helping his father catch a pony. As the spooked steed ran by, Will's father hurled a tomahawk to stop it. The hatchet struck Will's face, leaving that scar for life.

Protected behind bars in front of and to the left of Bligh is a living fossil, representing a great world botanic discovery. It is a Wollemi Pine (*Wollemia noblis*), dubbed the 'dinosaur tree', as fossils show it was widespread when Australia was part of the southern super continent Gondwana. Wollemies were thought to be long extinct until a grove of them was found in a secluded valley in the Wollemi National Park, only 150 km from Sydney, in 1994. The tree here was grown from seeds from one of those now-protected survivors. Wollemies continued to thrive in their valley during the ice age some 10,000 years ago when sea levels were 100 metres lower than today, when Sydney Harbour was a stream flowing to the ocean, which was about 20 km further west of Bondi Beach.

Sydney's base of sandstone was formed more than 200 million years ago when the area was a sea. The Cove was shaped about 6,000 years back. At the time of white settlement and before extensive reclamation, a little sandy beach near here punctuated a ledge of rock that held back the tide.

![30]

A bronze Captain William Bligh of the Bounty mutiny, navigator and Governor at the time of the Rum Rebellion, looking over Sydney Cove.

Sydney Cove still had a pastoral flavour, with slums nearby, in 1853 when F.C. Terry drew this illustration of the Tank Stream looking to Circular Quay from Hunter Street. Illustrated Sydney News, State Library of NSW.

SNAPSHOT 1788
An American in Paradise

SITTING ALONE in the longboat, American-born sailor Jacob Nagle cast a fishing line over the side. He was waiting patiently for the party lead by Captain Arthur Phillip to return. They were scrambling over the rocky foreshore to examine the sparkling little stream they had spotted as they rowed into this pristine and tranquil cove.

Jacob was the boat keeper. He had to stay behind to ensure that the boat was safe. He felt a nibble on the line, but whatever it was did not take the bait.

He looked at the twisting, knotty trees growing from crevices in the sandstone. He caught a glimpse of the blue and red coats of the officers and marines as they walked around a rocky ledge and disappeared again. Across the calm waters of what Lieutenant James Cook had called Port Jackson, Jacob Nagle could see two other longboats. One was skirting the northern shore, also in search of a good water supply and a place for a settlement. The other was being rowed down the middle of this nearly-landlocked harbour as a communication link.

Yes, nearly landlocked … and beautiful. Nagle had even overheard Capt'n Phillip tell an officer he thought it was one of the finest harbours in the world. A thousand ships could anchor here in perfect safety. Nagle agreed. This was the third day they had searched for another location for the settlement. Botany Bay, where the fleet was at anchor, did not live up to Phillip's hopes. The bay was incredibly open to strong winds and it was not deep. The soil was sandy. It was swampy in places … not good for the health of the new arrivals.

A nibble again. Then the line pulled against his index finger. Jacob gave a quick jerk. It was hooked! Slowly he pulled in the line, to boat a large black bream. He was delighted. He tossed it into the longboat's stern sheet.

Jacob was about to try for another one when he saw the party returning. He wound up the line and had placed it under his seat when Phillip arrived at the rock ledge where the craft was moored. Phillip was about to step aboard when he saw the fish. "Who caught that?" he asked. Jacob's face flushed. Capt'n Phillip rarely spoke to ordinary seamen, even though the American was the boat keeper. "I did," said Jacob Nagle, unsure of the repercussions. "Recollect," said Phillip with a smile, "that you are the first white man to catch a fish in Sydney Cove, where the town is to be built". So, this was where they would settle! Jacob liked the place.

NOTE: Your fishermen author has lately seen people catching black bream beside the ferry wharves at Circular Quay, only 100 metres from where Jacob Nagle caught that historic beauty. In recent years, whales have come into Sydney Harbour to cavort. Sure signs, they are, that the harbour is recovering after generations of awful pollution.

THE ROCKS is where the convicts were brought ashore from ships of the First Fleet to set up tents and other crude shelters. The military, the few free settlers and the Governor's administration people set up on the gentler and treed eastern side and also at the head of the cove, east of the Tank Stream. In fact, officialdom still hangs out there.

Some convicts thought this land in the mysterious antipodes, so far from home, was near China, on the same landmass and off to the west somewhere. And being in China, they reckoned, could be no worse than here. In 1792, 44 men and four women convicts bolted and headed west on foot for China. They were not heard of again; killed by natives or perished from hunger. Their mates assumed the bolters had made it to the land of the dragon. There is a reliable record of one scarpering convict who unknowingly walked in a big circle and unwittingly on the way back into Sydney confronted the notorious Major George Johnston (see page 74). "How did you get here in China?" the felon wondered, before he was shackled. He might have been the one who took with him, so as not to get lost, a drawing of a compass!

With no real welfare or hygienic services, no garbage facilities at first and the colony's economy stalled, The Rocks became a deep pocket of poverty, rife with crime, littered with brothels, gambling dens, opium dens (which were then legal), and grog shops purveying gut-wrenching spirits distilled locally. Only rain washed away human waste. The stink of the place, with no soil in which to dig cesspits, sometimes pervaded the whole of Sydney Cove. A snobby correspondent to *The Sydney Morning Herald* in 1858 called The Rocks Sydney's social cesspool and an "habitual resort of vicious and filthy humanity, from which the malaria of crime and disease incessantly arises and taints the social atmosphere".

31 Continuing our Walk, cross the little park from the Wollemi pine to a quaint Georgian residence two stories high. This is **Cadmans Cottage**, one of Sydney's oldest surviving buildings. A beach and shingles once extended nearly to the front door of the cottage, which the NSW National Parks and Wildlife Service administers well as a public attraction.

The rich to the east and the wretches shall go west. The enduring effects of Governor Phillip's decree in 1788 that the administration and private citizens camp among the trees on the gentler eastern side of Sydney Cove and the convicts to the steep western shore, The Rocks, is shown in this 1870 photograph. Charles Pickering. Mitchell Library, State Library of NSW.

Sydney traffic snarls are not new. Merchants' carts cram George Street, looking south from near the GPO c. 1899. Mitchell Library, State Library of NSW.

It is open every day except Good Friday and Christmas Day through the door at the rear. Also go into the basement facing Sydney Cove to see the building's excavated original stone footings.

Cadmans Cottage was built in 1816 as part of the Government Dockyard to accommodate its coxswain, the man in charge of government boats and their crews that took officials and workers around the Harbour, even up to Parramatta, and also convicts to their work stations. The third and longest-serving coxswain and Superintendent of Boats was John Cadman, who lived upstairs in the cottage now named after him until he retired in 1837.

The Water Police moved into Cadmans Cottage in the mid 1840s. The premises became a Court of Petty Sessions in 1849 and was extended to a design by Colonial Architect Mortimer Lewis to include offices and prison cells. The building continued as a police lockup until it was given to the Sydney Sailors' Home Trust to accommodate sailors taking a break from their ships. This kept the boys safer from the 'unscrupulous and immoral' private sailors' homes that were notorious in every port.

John Eyre's impression of Sydney Cove in 1810, six years before Cadmans Cottage was built. The flag and windmill are on Windmill Hill, above The Rocks. Mitchell Library, State Library of NSW

32 Take the pedestrian crossing over George Street. The impressive old sandstone building facing us, squeezed between more modern erections at 127 George Street, is on the site of the first general hospital in Australia, which functioned for 28 years. It began as tents for the sick the week the First Fleet arrived. A garden was planted to grow vegetables for those who arrived with scurvy. The modest hospital's builders were convicts. Productive Government Architect James Barnet then designed this carefully-carved gem to be **The Rocks Police Station,** which operated from 1882 until 1974.

The morsel in the jaws of the carved lion above the arched stone and Italianate Palladian-style watergate entrance is a police baton. The building now retails souvenirs.

For all this area's ribaldry in the 1800s and early 1900s, officialdom had little tolerance of people having a lively night on the town. In September 1834, one John Askmore, described in court as an 'assigned person' (a convict), was arrested when police found him after lawful trading hours in a house (a pub, we assume) at Fraziers Lane. He was convicted of "tripping on the light fantastic toe, to the tune Britons never will be slaves". Askmore's fun night copped him 36 lashes.

The author recommends going a few doors south of the old police station to have a look at the small Fortune of War Hotel. Your author likes to meet the locals at its island bar. The tales are sometimes historic but the décor is more 1900s Federation.

The original Fortune of War Inn was built in 1828, according to the sign in front, making this Sydney's oldest surviving pub. But several public houses make that sort of claim. You will sense now that The Rocks has a flavour quite different from the more establishment parts of Sydney where we have strolled so far.

The treat in the mouth of the carved lion over the entrance is a police baton.

VR

127

The former Rocks Police Station, on the site of
the colony's first tent hospital, in George Street.

33

Don't miss Suez Canal, the once-spooky old lane just before the Phillips Foote restaurant in George Street.

Just south from the Fortune of War, at 143a George with its distinctive old circular tower on the corner with Globe Street, is The Russell, which is now a boutique hotel and restaurant. This elegant establishment, claiming a history of drinkers at the site since 1790, was a thriving tavern run by former convict Samuel Terry in the early 1800s. He was one of many ex-con publicans in Old Sydney. The Russell was the Patent Slip Inn in 1880s, then the Port Jackson Hotel into the 1900s.

33 Back north about 80 paces beyond the old police station, just before No 101, the Phillip's Foote restaurant, and a few doors before the Sydney Cove Newsagency, is easily-missed **Suez Canal**. It got this moniker in the 1870s because, after heavy rain, it channeled a torrent of water down to George Street. Do enter this paved lane, single file, for a treat. It is one of the last of the many narrow alleys, or slypes, at The Rocks. They, along with stinking open drains, were declared dangerous and unhygienic and were mostly demolished or built over after the Bubonic Plague, or Black Death, outbreak of 1900.

The walls of the lane have characteristic signs that tell of when in the late 1800s and early 1900s Suez Canal was a haunt of dandily-dressed but dangerous gangs, often under jaunty high hats. Most gangs were called Pushes. Some gang names were based on their claimed territories, which they protected viciously. Others were determined by race. The gangs included The Rocks Push, the Argyle Cut Push, The Dawes Point Push, the Woolloomooloo Push, the Livers (who worked at the abattoirs), the Cabbage Tree Mob who wore colonial cabbage tree hats, and roving little mobs of Americans and Chinese. Gangs of rival Irish were the Orange Push and the Green Push. Push women were called Donahs.

They became known as larrikins, larking around, but they were also predatory robbers, bashers and killers mostly of lone pedestrians at night out of cruelty and/or the chance of stealing valuables. Weapons of the pushes included cut-throat razors, knives, spikes in the toes of their boots, and coshes in the form of socks of wet sand. This prompted the universal term, 'Sock it to 'em'. Some of the larrikins had pieces of mirror adhered to their boots so they could see up women's dresses.

They waged feuds, which the police were happy to ignore. At times battles raged around The Rocks between the pushes, mobs of seamen and scruffs from the army who were armed with belts studded with metal. The gangs waned from 1914 when many of their members left to fight in World War I. More about the pushes later.

34 Although it continues west past Nurses Walk to Harrington Street, turn right from Suez Canal to enter a wondrous little courtyard reeking with history. A two story former residence on your left is believed to be the oldest surviving authentic cottage in The Rocks. It is younger than Cadmans Cottage, but has its original walls, window frames and 1829 banister up to the bedroom.

The cottage's builder and long-time resident was Irish blacksmith and life-sentence convict William Reynolds, evidently a tough old character of The Rocks. He had an illegal 'ratting pit' where punters bet on how many rats a terrier could kill in five minutes. Also, a dig in 1989 revealed evidence of organised cock, cat and dog fights.

34

Greenway Lane, the cobbled bower near where architect Francis Greenway lived.

Suez Canal was called Reynolds Lane in the mid 1800s. A feature here is a well of sandstone six metres deep, dating from about 1820.

The Rocks once had hundreds like it. It was discovered full of trash and animal skeletons under an ancient dunny by an archeological dig. No doubt blacksmith Bill Reynolds spent time here yarning with his immediate eastern neighbour for some years, convicted forger and the colony's first architect, Francis Greenway.

Take the steps down some 20 metres, past excellent culinary centres, beside palms and with sunlight dappling through gnarled trees on a sunny day, is a coarsely-cobbled walkway known as Greenway Lane, after of course the former illustrious architect resident who once lived here.

35 Leaving Greenway Lane brings us to that part of Argyle Street, once the hub of a meat market, that was landscaped with boxed shrubbery and made a shared pedestrian and vehicle way in 2008 and named in recognition of the man most agree is the saviour of much of Sydney's built heritage as we know it, **Jack Mundey Place**.

Your author has studied many differing accounts of 'the troubles' of the time and has talked with people who were involved; Jack Mundey, other activists and former policemen. Indeed, as a newspaper reporter your author was there at the time.

In the late 1960s and early 1970s, developers sniffed a fortune awaiting them by pulling down the jumble of The Rocks and building plush complexes, with marinas for the pleasure boats of the wealthy.

The State Government supported them, wanting to modernise in a sort of harmony with the Opera House and other new developments east of Sydney Cove. Big money, wanting more money, was going to win. The losers would be long-time local residents.

The Rocks Residents Action Group's Secretary, the late Nita McCrea, asked several organisations to help them fight against the demolitions. An unlikely ally strode forth: the Builders Labourers Federation (BLF), led by Jack Mundey, its colourful, radical left-wing Secretary. Jack coined the term 'Green Ban' on any construction in the area, which he imposed with immutable conviction.

The saviour of the built heritage of The Rocks and other parts of Sydney, then Builders Labourers Federation Secretary Jack Mundey, being arrested while demonstrating against the demolition of the Playfair Building at The Rocks in 1973. Jack coined the term Green Ban. Part of Argyle Street is now the walker-friendly Jack Mundey Place. Sydney Morning Herald.

He told a crowd, "There must be provision for working class people to reside … there will never, ever, be any reconstruction, any rejuvenation of this area until such time as the residents receive iron-clad guarantees that people in the lower income brackets, workers, can afford to live in these areas." This from a union whose members would get a lot of employment from demolitions and building.

Green Ban supporters sat on, and refused to leave, the roofs of buildings and perched like possums in old trees in Argyle Street. This attracted huge publicity, hence more public support, notably when in 1973 Jack was arrested and hauled off to jail from near today's Jack Mundey Place.

Eventually, the Green Bans won what became known as 'The Battle for The Rocks'. The bans were lifted after the Government compromised with its People's Plan and built the big Sirius Apartment comples on Cumberland Street for cheap residential rentals.

Other government measures protected the environment and allowed better consideration of the public in matters of planning and heritage.

The Rocks has survived, notwithstanding the place being pretty well surrounded with newish buildings today and many former homes becoming offices and shops. Jack's BLF saved many other parts of Old Sydney and other Australian cities from destruction.

The Sydney Harbour Foreshore Authority established Jack Mundey Place. It is responsible for restoring links with this area's past, conserving its early buildings to ensure at least another century of use. As part of its Jack Mundey Place recognition, the Authority has installed three panels in adjoining Kendall Lane, the site of the protests, commemorating the Green Bans era. The panels, the Authority advises, are to put the bans in their broader, more important, context. We should note that there are still pockets of confusion between what was proposed in 1973 and models of an even more dastardly demolition job canvassed in 1967.

Jack Mundey's actions marshalled the workers as well as the enlightened middle classes. He pioneered organised public action to preserve the urban environment, even in Europe and the United States. And that inspired the name of the world's influential Greens political parties. Still proudly a radical left-winger, Jack is also still a passionate protector of our built heritage. He was

The Rocks' representative alderman on the City of Sydney Council (1984–87), an executive member of the Australian Conservation Foundation for 20 years to 1993, and Chair of the NSW Historic Houses Trust from 1995 to 2001. He was awarded honorary doctorates at the University of NSW and Sydney University and made an Officer of Order of Australia. Thanks, mate.

Stephen Lane, a constable aged 19 at Jack's arrest, wrote to the Geographic Names Board urging the naming of Jack Mundey Place. Former nemesis Stephen, who saw the light, is credited with influencing the Place's establishment.

36 Continuing our walk, an important primary visit is across Jack Mundey Place and through an arcade between Playfair Street and Kendall Lane to **The Sydney Visitor Centre** upstairs. The staff, and heaps of free brochures, can give you a detailed guide to what's going on around here and also information about visitor attractions, tours, shopping and accommodation. The Centre also has an excellent shop selling books and Australian souveniers.

Part Five
The Rocks Museum, Dawes Point, The Coathanger

AHEAD IS THE CORE of The Rocks, an amazing prophesy, the Aboriginal track that became the colony's High Street and how the Sydney Harbour Bridge was built and dramatically opened.

37 FROM THE VISITOR CENTRE, take the stairs down to cobbled Kendall Lane. A few paces away across the lane is **The Rocks Discovery Museum**, a highlight of our Walk with free, fascinating and fun activities of an historical bent for all the family. Another attraction from the Sydney Harbour Foreshore Authority, it is in three sandstone buildings built over 10 years from 1844.

A feature of the museum is an interactive display of this precinct's history from pre-European times, through the 1788 to 1820 colony days, the development of the port from 1820 to 1900 and then the transformations from 1900 on. It is an entertaining and informative creation. The museum shop has a fine range of books, branded merchandise, kids' games and authentic Aboriginal artefacts and artworks.

Back in Kendall Lane, where the Green Bans information signs are, return to Jack Mundey Place in Argyle Street. Please resist an urge to turn right to the looming Argyle Cut. We will be there later. Turn left at the 1844 Orient Hotel, the façade of which has been restored to nearly as it was when it first became a pub in the mid 1800s. A regular retreat for meat workers and sailors, the hotel was formerly named the Marine, Buckinghams, Mays Family Hotel and Pries Family Hotel. It has been The Orient since 1884

Turn left at the corner and stroll north along George Street. This is surely the most colourful part of the most history-packed street in Sydney. It was the settlement's first street, really a rough foot track probably formed for millennia by the Cadigal people who did not need fires

The Orient Hotel and (opposite) George St at the junction of Argyle St, The Rocks.

Old Sydney's original wharf was behind the verandahed Australian Hotel, George Street, in the late 1800s. The single-storey building left of the hotel was a fire station.

to cook fish and birds' eggs on the rocks around here in hot weather. It extended between rows of tents and later government houses and other buildings to the gun battery near today's southern pylons of the bridge. As the area's main thoroughfare, called High Street until 1810, pubs, merchants' storehouses and shops began to replace the early structures. Pickpockets and better-off colonials on horseback mixed with a rising population of dogs and cats and European rats, stowaways from ships in the Cove. It was, of course, Governor Macquarie, with his usual disregard for local custom, who named it George Street to honour King George III. It is one of many Australian places Macquarie named after his ultimate boss.

Horse and cart traffic soon formed ruts and cracks in the sandstone, so the street was paved with blocks from ironbark eucalypt trees from 1888 until the 1930s. Some of the blocks remain under today's asphalt. But a lot were stolen and used as firewood.

38 As you see, a goodly number of the buildings on each side of George Street retain their old facades. Across the street from the 1909 Federation-styled Observer Hotel, the author, as a young reporter, remembers the verandahed brick building at 102 George, now a craft gallery, as the **Coroner's Court and City Morgue**, stacked with drawers of the dead. Next door at No. 100 was the 1856 Mariner's Church, a heritage icon which the Sydney Harbour Foreshore Authority has refurbished. Quick wealth lured a lot immigrants to NSW, including the beautiful entertainer Lola Montez, ex-mistress of that fearsome whipper of newspaper editors, Ludwig of Bavaria. Lola also flayed with a whip a critical editor, Henry Seekamp of *The Ballarat Times*, Victoria. She once confounded a Sydney process server by stripping off all her clothes and daring him to seize her. He fled.

Sailors galore jumped ship at the Cove and strode west in search of gold. Ships were left stranded with depleted crews. This escalated shanghaiing and press ganging of (usually drunk) young men who awoke on ships at sea. No one had much interest then in a person (assumed drunk) being lugged or wheelbarrowed through the streets. You may have heard or read about clandestine tunnels from pubs to the waterfront used by kidnappers and smugglers at The Rocks. They are fanciful myths. There were no such tunnels. The stone around here was too tough, as the convict diggers found out at the Argyle Cut.

Gentrified Dawes Point c. 1855, looking south from the junction of George Street with Cumberland Street rising in the middle, and Lower Fort Street behind the street lamp. Left, the Harbour View Hotel. Dixson Galleries, State Library of NSW.

SNAPSHOT 1852

Gold diggers dream as their women weep

SHE CLENCHED her eyes to disassociate herself from the abhorrent act. Where was he? Where was that stupid husband of hers? Oh yes, everything will be fine and dandy, he had said. We'll start a new life in a new country. Everything will be wonderful. You wait and see. John had promised her a lovely house … possibly a cottage, with a garden. There would be plenty of work for decent folk. Good wages, too.

Reluctantly, she had given in to his desire, uprooted their lives, left her family and friends behind. And spent five months in a damp, smelly shipboard cabin going to the ends of the earth. Cabin? It was more like one of them convict cells!

Suddenly his stinking breath made her whirl her head to the side. When will it end? When they arrived in Sydney Town she and John were amazed. They did not expect to see such a thriving town and that beautiful harbour. Yes, she had thought to herself, perhaps they had done the right thing. Perhaps things would be all right. And they were, for a while. He found a job. Not the best job but an honest job, with regular wages. They found lodgings. Not that cottage he had promised but it was a roof over their heads.

They resided in The Rocks and it was not the most salubrious part of the settlement. Over the months, they had learned to turn a blind eye to the goings on. Only two doors away was a sly grog-shop with people coming and going at day and night. And they were so boisterous! Next to the grog-shop was a joss house where people smoked opium. She had seen some strange people going into that place. Some very prominent too. And on the other side of the joss house was that bawdy house, its painted women all tarted up. All smiles, those women are! Giving the sailors the 'come on'. Giving up their bodies to … The thought snapped her back to reality. When was he going to finish! Why did it have to come to this! Oh, where are you, John? When will you come home?

Yes, life had been reasonably good until it happened! It was a whisper that grew into a roar. The word was on everyone's lips … Gold! She had tried to hold him back as John's workmates ran off to their Eldorado. She convinced him that they were only rumours.

No one could pick pieces of gold from the ground. It was a myth. Then some returned with nuggets. John fled the next day with gold fever without a thought for the three children, or me. How would we live? There were no jobs for women. Except for this. She looked at the five shillings he had just put on the bedside table. And wept.

39

Once the HQ of The Australasian Steam Navigation Co. under its pyramid spire, this polychrome brick landmark in Hickson Road is on the site of Campbell's old mansion and the premises of Australia's second bank, established in 1819 to encourage convicts to bank their earnings.

OUR WALK continues to the right off George Street, down Hickson Road, named after the Chairman of the Sydney Harbour Trust 1901-13. Past the Ken Done Gallery and Trend Imports is a grand old building at the corner leading to the Overseas Passenger Terminal.

39 This was the site of Scots merchant Robert Campbell's mansion, Wharf House. His gabled and austere sandstone former warehouse stands at 11 to 31 Hickson Road. The **Australasian Steam Navigation Co**. bought the corner property in 1876. It commissioned architect William Wardell to design today's five-level warehouse of brick with Flemish-style gables and a campanile topped with a tapered pyramid spire. Australia's second bank, The Savings Bank of NSW, also known as "Campbell's Bank", was established here in 1819 to encourage convicts to bank their earnings.

Take the steps to the left of the passenger terminal to Campbell Cove, with a good view of the Opera House. Many fine restaurants occupy former storehouses on the left. Continue along this sublime part of the waterfront, past the Park Hyatt Hotel, to grassy Hickson Road Reserve at Dawes Point.

40 Cross Hickson Road to Dawes Point Park and take the path up to the southern end of the **Sydney Harbour Bridge**, the world landmark and brilliant feat of engineering, probably roaring with traffic. The architect and chief engineer throughout the project was Dr. J. J. C. Bradfield. Affectionately known as 'The Coathanger', the bridge's 485,000 square metres of steelwork would cover 60 football fields. It is based on the design of New York's much smaller Hell Gate Bridge.

Sydney should be irked to learn that New York's Bayonne Bridge, being constructed at the same time, was extended deliberately to make it longer than the Sydney Harbour Bridge, by half a metre! The Sydney Harbour Bridge is more than half a kilometre long and 134 metres above sea level. Held together by six million rivets, it carries 57 million vehicles, plus trains, a year.

A punt took passengers across the harbour from here until, after years of waiting, widespread betting on whether the arms of the arches would actually meet, the bridge was officially opened on 19 March 1932.

Those who bet the arches would meet now look likely winners! No bridge there yet but this progress was hailed throughout the city in the Depression year of 1930, two years before the bridge's dramatic opening. Mitchell Library, State Library of NSW.

Sydney Harbour Bridge modern day, looking east.

Captain de Groot, after he "opened" the bridge.

The event was a shambles. A huge crowd had gathered, a ribbon was strung across the southern end of the bridge to be ceremoniously cut after the politicians' speeches, when a nutter and officer of the right-wing New Guard, Captain de Groot, spurred his horse to the ribbon and, with the second underhand swipe of his sword, cut the ribbon. "On behalf of the decent and loyal citizens of New South Wales, I declare the bridge open!" he cried. With a foot caught in a stirrup, he fell to the ground as police dragged him from the saddle. De Groot was fined £5 and spent a few days in jail.

Botanist and philosopher Erasmus Darwin, grandfather of evolutionist and voyager to Sydney, Charles Darwin, penned an amazing prophesy about the Sydney Harbour Bridge only a year after white settlement. Inspired by stories of the new colony in the antipodes, Erasmus in England wrote a poem *Visit of Hope to Sydney Cove*. His allegorical figure Hope, 143 years before completion of The Coathanger, described the future scene of Sydney:

> There the proud arch, Colossus-like, bestride Yon glittering streams, and
> bound the chafing tide …

The bridge comes alive, sparkling with colourful lights and fireworks at night nowadays to celebrate important events.

Marines Lieutenant and astronomer William Dawes set up a tent and a basic astronomical observatory here soon after the First Fleet dropped anchor in 1788. The five 1840s cannon of iron arrayed under the bridge, taking a bead on the Harbour, are reminders of the Dawes Point Battery of guns, and later fort, dating back to 1791. It was demolished in 1925 to make way for the bridge.

The fortification was built to protect Sydney from feared invasions from the sea by the Russians, French and even Americans when Britain, thus also this colony, was at war with those countries. But the cannon never fired a shot in anger. The soldiers based here and elsewhere in the colony, incidentally, had flintlock muskets which would take two alternative types of flint to place in their hammers. The cheap outer-skin flintstone never lasted long. Denser, more costly, stone lasted longer. So those using the expensive stuff called those using cheap skin stone, skinflints. The insult, describing a mean and niggardly person, has endured.

Rat hunters caught more than 100,000 rats at The Rocks during the bubonic plague in 1900. The plague was carried by the rats' fleas. State Archives of NSW.

Part Six

A pissoir, the rat slaughter, Argyle Cut

DIGNIFIED TERRACE HOUSES, grottos cut in the rocks for shanty houses, a massive rat hunt and the true tale of an encounter with The Argyle Cut mob are ahead.

FROM UNDER THE BRIDGE, stroll to the end of Lower Fort Street, which led to the Dawes Point Battery and named after the military fort that was never completed on Flagstaff Hill to the south.

The street is graced on its western side by a row of elegant Georgian and Victorian terrace houses of three and four levels built for middle-class citizens from the 1830s. Up until quite recently, the terraces were rented to public housing tenants by the NSW government, however recently some of the buildings have been sold ostensibly to fund more public housing in much needed areas outside of the inner city. However, many residents argue that the public housing tenants have been slowly pushed out as the suburb becomes more gentrified.

This is our first look at the top of The Rocks, an obviously more refined district than where the lowlifes lived down nearer Sydney Cove.

Stroll south by the park and then into the end of George Street to our left by the popular 1921 Harbour View Hotel. Continue past an ornate and historic public toilet, or pissoir in the French style, made of cast iron, and under the road to the bridge.

The 1915 Mercantile Hotel on the right, on the corner at the end of Gloucester Walk, is one of the city's fine traditional pubs. It features green tiles on the lower walls that were once commonplace. The tiles, often in bars along with stone and concrete floors that replaced earlier dirt and sawdust, were easy to hose down after a busy night. Quaint old terrace-house shops past the pub are worth inspecting.

Turn right off George Street into Atherden Street. The big Georgian building of three levels at the corner on the right is the former Union Bond

Store, now the Westpac Bank and Museum we can enter off Atherden Street. If you happen to like money, it presents the story of legal tender in Australia, exhibiting old notes and coins including the holey dollar.

See the windows that never were? This style of faux (or false) window spaces was a Georgian vogue, bringing to mind a strange episode in the heady history of taxation. In 1696, long before they thought of income tax, Britain imposed a greedy window or glass tax by which the King was paid yearly for every window in every private building in the land. The tax caused many folk to replace glass in their windows with timber and stone. Faux windows later became fashionable, regardless of the window tax, even in colonial Australia. The tax inspired the expression Daylight Robbery.

The bond store's false windows obviously were never intended to have glass, as fireplaces are located behind them. The Old Sydney Holiday Inn building on the other Atherden Street corner was an early marvellous restoration project by the (now) Sydney Harbour Foreshore Authority so it blended with this spot's historic flavour. The original part of the brick building here went up in 1925, replacing ancient stores and terraces.

41 Graphic carvings on the intriguing **First Impressions** monument before us present the colony's history. Carvings on different faces of the monument tell the stories of the first immigrant settlers, the convicts and the soldiers. We can thank for that the Sydney Harbour Foreshore Authority and the Fellowship of First Fleeters.

Ahead in dead-end Atherden Street, leading to some palms and a wall of hewn stone, is a captivating little row of private terrace homes on its left side dating to the 1870s or 80s.

42 Turn left into Playfair Street with its many fine restaurants and shops. Two doorways past the offices of The Rocks Walking Tours, turn right into a passageway through the building facing the street, to face across a little courtyard by a **wall carved into a ridge of rock**. Grottos were hewn here as sheds, laundries and lavatories in the 1880s at the rear of the terraces.

This is our best confrontation with the bare rocks of The Rocks. Stairs across

Market Day at Playfair Street, The Rocks. The monument honouring The Settlers, the Soldiers and The Convicts was commisioned by the Sydney Harbour Foreshore Authority and presented by the Fellowship of First Fleeters.

the courtyard take us to another level with relics and steel reproductions of modest colonial furnishings. They commemorate hovels here built from 1874 to 1880 with walls of natural rock. At least the sheerness of the place and the solid stone resulted in rains flushing away refuse from the yards and streets, but often into the homes below. And even the folk living near the top of this staggered ridge copped distain (and smelly refuse) from the relative gentility residing above them.

The Rocks' first sewerage system came in stages from 1857 but, thanks to landlords who declined to pay for maintenance, it was generally in a bad state by 1900 when Bubonic Plague, the Black Death, hit Sydney.

Near hysteria swept the settlement. A little-known related medical achievement in Australia was by Drs John Ashburton Thompson and Frank Tidswell. They pursued from a laboratory on Goat Island a theory by Frenchman P.L.G. Simond in 1898 that fleas carried the disease to humans from rats. Rats that, in Sydney's case, were stowaways on ships from other plague-infected ports. The Australians proved that Simond was correct, showing Sydney how to combat the plague and also earning gratitude from the rest of the world.

A big rat slaughter followed. A bounty of two pence (about two cents) a head was soon boosted to six pence a head. Six pence was handy pocket money then. It attracted teams of professional ratters. The potential bonanza of money caused some residents to become rat farmers for rich rewards. Children were some of the keenest rat catchers, probably copping some fleas. 108,000 rats were consigned to incinerators during the plague. Authorities seized the opportunity as an excuse to buy up the haphazard wharves and warehouses and redevelop Sydney as a model of port development. At the same time, the Government bought houses and businesses of the area, claiming them to be substandard and disease-ridden. The intention was to build a sort of workers' paradise for people employed on the new wharves. But by the time the Black Death had passed, only three of its 165 victims in Australia, 103 of them in Sydney, were residents of The Rocks and adjoining Millers Point.

The studio of artist Egon Huch, aged 85, who can paint your portrait on the spot and has worked at The Rocks for over 35 years, is a grotto in the cliff face off Playfair Street.

The boy on The Rocks, about 1900. Government Printing Office Collection, State Library of NSW.

43 More steps go up to Gloucester Walk. Turn left and take the ancient stairs down to Argyle Street and the famous **Argyle Cut**. Gangs of convicts from the Hyde Park Barracks, some of them serious criminals in chains, cut at the Cut from the east and west for two years from 1843 as a needed channel for traffic to and from wharves to the west. They hewed the solid rock with hand picks and hammers as an early engineering achievement in the colony. Convicts also dug Busby's Bore to Hyde Park and filled in Circular Quay, where we walked earlier. Convicts carted the rubble by hand cart from The Cut to the Quay for landfill over the mudflats by the Tank Stream.

The horror job was made tougher by the 'supervision' of notorious sadist and bully officer Timothy Lane. "By the help of God and the strong arm of the flogger," he once yelled, "you'll get 50 before breakfast tomorrow". Lane had a chair installed in the Barracks' yard from which he cheered on his floggers. The rock was too tough for the convicts and their tools to complete The Cut. Paid labourers using gunpowder finished the gap and widened it for more traffic over a few years until 1864. Other work followed in the 1900s. Machines used in this work made grooves you might see in the walls, not convict picks. The Cut was first bridged by timber, then stone. The highway above it now goes to and from the Harbour Bridge.

43

The Argyle Cut, narrower than it is today, in 1870. Mitchell Library, State Library of NSW.

Newly arrived seaman Elliott Johnson captured this pencil drawing of the character and characters of The Rocks in 1883. Johnson became a Federal MP and was knighted in 1920. Mitchell Library, State Library of NSW.

SNAPSHOT 1899
"What's up, fellers?": the Argyle Cut Mob!

HE STARED into the darkness. Would it be safe? Or should he take the long way around? The young cove in a suit, whom we shall call Jimmy Walker, didn't think the meeting at the Garrison Church would take so long as it did. Now darkness had engulfed Sydney. Gas lamps tried to light the dangerous narrow road through the Argyle Cut.

Yes, dangerous. But was it too early for the gangs of larrikins to be roaming the streets and alleyways of The Rocks? Could he make it to Circular Quay without being accosted? Foolishly, he strode to the Cut.

A movement in the darkness caught Walker's eye. Shadows of human form moved towards him. He faced his foe, but a noise made him swing on his heels. More members of the infamous Argyle Cut Mob were closing in. Walker scrutinized his nemeses. Their leering faces under hats on the back of their heads showed greasy hair.

They wore short waistcoats and flared pants that covered boots with heels so high that some of the mobsters seemed to be unsteady on their feet. What worried Walker, though, were the pointy toes of their boots, ready to bruise his muscles and break his ribs.

Some carried socks packed with wet sand. These were the mobs' favourite weapons; coshes that from one blow could strike a man senseless but were easily disposed of so police could not use them in a prosecution. There were at least 40 in the silent mob; too close for him to run. Only last week he had read in *The Sydney Morning Herald* about someone being kicked to death by the Argyle Cut Mob. Would he make the next edition?

Jimmy's only option was to bluff them. He tipped his hat back and lifted his head to expose a forced smile. "What's up fellers?" he exclaimed. As the light of a gas lamp fell on his face, two of his accosters lit up with smiles.

"That's Mr Walker, the solicitor!" one announced. "He's got Jimbo off. Stand down boys." Jimmy remembered defending a larrikin a few weeks before. The gang disappeared into the darkness to await another victim. But the two who recognised him closed in on each side of him. They were his bodyguards down through the neighbouring Push gang's quarter. At the Quay, one gave instructions that would sear in young Jimmy Walker's memory. "Never do that again," he warned. "You could have been kicked to death."

44 A final visit on this part of our Walk we recommend is just down Argyle Street and through the high-arched stone doorway to the big **Argyle Store**. It was built from 1826 as a vast commercial centre, spreading from the mansion of Sydney's Harbour Master, Captain John Piper. The Old Argyle Bond here, with vast cellars still in use, was the heart of the empire of former convict girl Mary Reibey, whose servant and bodyguard then was the giant Fijian woman, Feefoo. Archibald Mosman's whaling station warehouse was here around here, too. The complex became an important wine store and is now mostly a thriving restaurant.

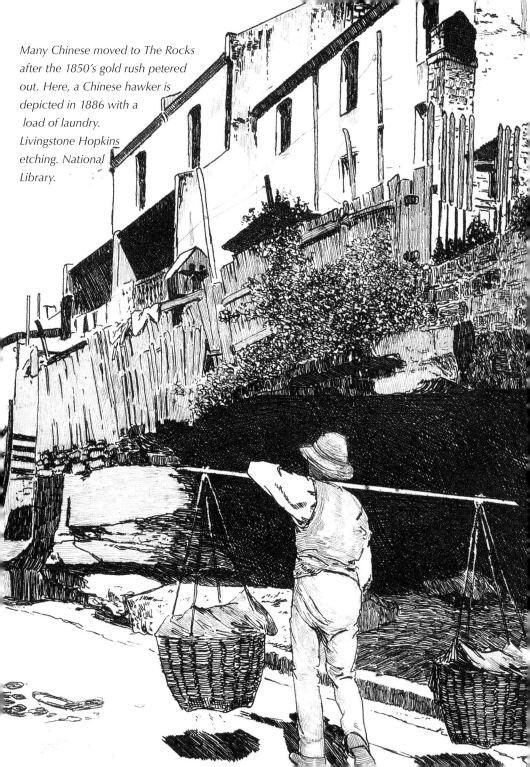

Many Chinese moved to The Rocks after the 1850's gold rush petered out. Here, a Chinese hawker is depicted in 1886 with a load of laundry. Livingstone Hopkins etching. National Library.

Children, their mums and grannies turned out in their best finery for this picture taken where they lived in Cambridge Street, The Rocks, in 1901, soon after the Bubonic Plague. Mitchell Library, State Library of NSW.

Part Seven

Susannah Place, gangster murder, the Observatory

PLACES ALONG HERE give you a real taste of working-class life in the 1800s, we visit a heritage hotel, there's a chance to top the Harbour Bridge and to view the heavens through historic 'scopes.

CROSS ARGYLE STREET just east of the Argyle Cut and venture up Cambridge Street. The pedestrian way has little of the character of the colourful cottages that once graced this place. But after about 150 metres we come to the back fences through and over which we can see some little colonial back yards, with traditional-style clothes lines, belonging to rows of terrace houses facing the street above.

A Place in The Rocks, 1902. Sophie Steffanoni's oil painting captures the morning mood of Cambridge Street, now "redeveloped". The Argyle Cut is at the end of the street. Caroline Simpson Library & Research Collection, Historic Houses Trust of NSW.

PART SEVEN

141

The back of the wonderful Susannah Place Museum, built in 1844.

45 Turn up the steps at the right at Cumberland Place. The terrace house on the junction with Gloucester Street is the endearing **Susannah Place Museum**, which your author rates as the best museum of working-class life in Old Sydney. As we can see through the windows, the door at the corner, where there is usually a cat or two, opens to a traditional Cheap Cash Grocer corner store styled and stocked much as it was in 1915. Jars of boiled lollies, fly paper, rolls of string, old-fashioned dolly pegs and a poster for Baldwins Herbal Blood Pills.

The museum opens on weekends and during school holidays for superb guided tours of an hour of this and three adjoining terrace houses of orange brick. The houses are furnished from basement kitchens with coal chutes to ground-floor living rooms to upstairs bedrooms as they were in the mid 1800s with tinkling echoes of ordinary life and dramas of generations of old, the Rileys and the Finnegans. But, surprisingly and unlike so many spooky places visited by The Rocks Ghost Tours, no ghosts, we're told.

The Place is named after Susannah Stern, the step daughter of an 1840s owner of the shop building, which had a good view of the Cove until the 1970s and luckily avoided demolition after the 1900 bubonic plague.

46 The long block of three-level residences once opposite, facing Gloucester Street, were not so lucky. They were obliterated. But ongoing archaeological excavations since 1994 have revealed a remarkable complex of **stone foundations** dating back to perhaps the late 1700s. Also, evidence of earlier occupation by the Cadigals, who called this area Warrane.

The Youth Hostels Association has built a hostel here that incorporates the archaeological remains of over 30 houses that stood here until 1911and which are kept visible to the public. The early laneways were uncovered during the excavations.

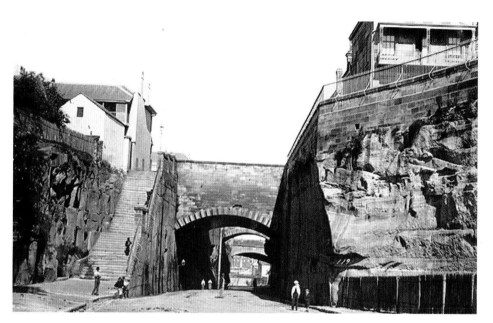

Ancient stairs that lead from Argyle Street to the famous Argyle Cut.

The skyline over The Rocks has changed a lot since this photo was taken in 1966. Gloucester Street colonial terraces face The Australian Heritage Hotel on the Cumberland Street corner. Aust. Photo Agency. Mitchell Library, State Library of NSW.

A Morton Bay fig tree frames the Sydney Harbour Bridge from Observatory Park.

47 Next door north on the corner with Cumberland Street is the outstanding wedge-shaped **Australian Heritage Hotel**. This place holds the original licence from the Australian Hotel, the sea captains' refined retreat in George Street for many years from 1824, as described in Part 5. This has justified another heritage claim for a Sydney hotel; to having the city's oldest licence.

No doubt two regulars at taverns around here were seafaring authors Joseph Conrad and Jack London. They lodged at premises near today's Australian, which I blushingly report is your author's base at The Rocks. In his book *The Cruise of the Snark*, London wrote how in 1907 the harbour master at Suva caused London to correct a navigation error, thus saving *Snark* from possibly hitting a reef. The Scots harbour master was Captain Charles Wooley, great grandfather of the *60 Minutes* reporter of the same name. Facilities at the Federation-style premises even include a ladies' parlour, still furnished as it probably was when the place was built in 1912. It replaced another Australian Hotel that was just south along Cumberland Street, on the archaeological site, from 1889 to 1911.

A plaque on the Gloucester Street side of the hotel marks the scene of one of Sydney's many unsolved underworld murders. In 1956, Cecil Dubois was the starting-price bookmaker at the Australian Hotel. Like hundreds of others plying this illegal business in Sydney, Dubois took bets of cash from punters on, mostly, horse races. Having plenty of money around, Dubois was a likely mark for John William Manners, a local hoodlum gunman. Manners, the story goes, stole £800 from Dubois' car parked near The Australian.

Not content with that, the crim then threatened Dubois at the hotel bar with a bashing unless the bookie handed over £50. Soon after, Manners was found shot dead on the footpath outside. A hard man, George Joseph Hackett (1922-1959), a mate of the bookie, was tried for murder and acquitted.

Cumberland Street is named after the Duke of Cumberland, Queen Victoria's wicked uncle. Quaint and gracious old town houses and cottages on the west side were demolished to make way for the approaches to the Sydney Harbour Bridge. Residents included Australia's first Prime Minister, Edmund Barton, and at No. 35 David Scott Mitchell, whose collection was the foundation of the Mitchell Library.

From The Australian Hotel, stroll across Gloucester Street and over the Argyle Cut to the old Glenmore Hotel, with lots of Federation character and offering grand views of Sydney and the Harbour from its roof-top beer garden and restaurant.

Cross to the western side of Cumberland Street for a great view from above the Argyle Cut. A little north is where, if you are sane and sober, are more than 1.2 metres tall and comply with other conditions, you can join a Sydney Harbour Bridge Climb to the top of the arch.

The Argyle Cut today, from Cumberland Street.

From The Cut crossing, go a little south and take the steps up to a pedestrian tunnel under the Bradfield Highway to an amazingly different side of Sydney, Millers Point. It is clothed here in trees in spacious parklands overlooking the bridge, the North Shore, the upper Harbour and the relatively sedate streets of the point. The top of the road before us, Upper Fort Street, was once home to the hallowed Fort Street High School where many of the nation's most prominent citizens were educated. The institution, whose scholars are called Fortians, was established in 1849 as a Model School in the former Military Hospital, commissioned by Governor Macquarie in 1815. In 1916 the Fort Street Boys' High was relocated to the suburb of Petersham; the Girls' High School remaining on Observatory Hill. The two schools were reunited at Petersham in 1975.

48 The street circles the old school to the Centre for the National Trust of Australia (NSW). Before us here is the outstanding **S. H. Ervin Gallery** of art, regularly displaying visiting exhibitions, an outstanding exhibitor to the public of historical and contemporary paintings, and a centre of research into the nation's art over the years. It is closed on Mondays and public holidays.

Philanthropist and collector Samuel Henry Ervin bequeathed the gallery's foundation display. Artists represented here include Arthur Streeton, Conrad Martens, Eugene von Guerard, Donald Friend, Nora Heysen, James Gleeson and Lloyd Rees.

49 Enter Observatory Park left and north of the gallery to the famous and domed **Sydney Observatory** of weathered sandstone blocks, run by the Powerhouse Museum. This pioneering centre of meteorological observation is open every day except Good Friday and Christmas Day. There are also tours at night when we can have a look at the universe through wondrous equipment. A popular attraction is the 3-D Space Theatre.

The Observatory was built in 1858 on the hexagonal foundations of the military's never-completed Phillip Fort. Governor King commissioned the fort in 1803 after an insurrection by convicts transported for fighting against England's occupation of Ireland. A staffed flag here from 1788 was seen from much of Sydney and by ships entering the Harbour. Governor Phillip posted a lookout by the flag on the hill so he would know when a ship entered The Heads. This gave it the name Flagstaff Hill, which changed to Windmill Hill when the Government had a windmill built here in 1797.

The Government Astronomer, who had famous predecessors you can read about, was based here until 1982, when the city's lights and pollution hampered astronomical observation. It became a museum, now packed with fascination and history, plus navigation devices and rare time pieces. The Observatory also has a fine book and souvenir shop and a café.

It's recommended leaving the Observatory from the southern side you probably entered by and take the path in a clockwise direction around the complex past superb Moreton Bay figs to an old cannon or iron and a memorial to "the volunteers from NSW who responded to the Empire's call to the South African War [the Boer War] 1899- 1902". A plaque informs us that 15 units of soldiers with 327 officers and 6,000 other ranks sailed to the war. 244 of those young men from the young nation, Federated during the conflict, were killed. Some had been members of pushes at The Rocks.

Nearby at this great spot for a picnic on the grass, perhaps naughtily feeding the birds, is a former band rotunda giving views to fire up any photographer. Walk down to the north-east corner of Observatory Park to the top of Watson Street to continue our Walk in a different sort of Old Sydney.

The growth of a city in a gross of years...The panorama of Sydney in 1864 and 2008, looking north from Observatory Hill, Millers Point.

Darling Harbour & Parramatta, North Shore, Sydney Harbour looking N.E., City.

Darling Harbour & Parramatta

1864 image, Freeman Bros & Prout 1864, stitched by Leo Carol from Mitchell Library prints. 2008 image, Christopher Shain, stitched by Leo Carol. Courtesy, National Trust of Aust. (NSW).

Part Eight

Garrison Church, Hero of Waterloo & Lord Nelson

AN HISTORIC CHURCH and taverns and the mixed lot who frequented them feature in our stroll ahead, along with a ghost, gracious old homes, a tale of a tunnel, Jack the Miller and a collection of funny pub names.

TURN LEFT and stroll north along Watson Street. Cross it about 100 metres on to go down some stairs of ancient stone cut in a cliff face to Argyle Street, west of the Cut. Pretty well from the beginnings of white settlement at Millers Point, it was a place of refinement compared with The Rocks on the other side of the stone ridge breached by the Cut. That difference remains. It is mostly residential. A goodly number of the homes were built for wealthy merchants, ship owners and other gentry. Plane, oak and Moreton Bay fig trees, with mynas, sparrows, blackbirds, gulls, pigeons, crows and parrots studding them like jewels, border some streets. Greenery tumbles from many a stone cliff and ancient wall.

This is a charming precinct unlike any other in Sydney. The architecture of buildings at Millers Point shows the styles of the ages over the past 220 years. Some humble shanties, timber conlonial to stone Georgian, Regency, Victorian, then Federation of the early 1900s, some art deco, to modern. Do stop and contemplate some of these mostly terraced structures, many of them with wrought iron lace at their balconies. They seem to whisper their tales of glory and drama.

50 Before us, across Argyle Street and facing the top of Lower Fort Street, is one of Sydney's most historic buildings, the **Garrison Church of the Holy Trinity**. It was the church for the British Red Coats of the 50th Queen's Own Regiment, garrisoned at the Dawes Battery down the street. Ships' masters and seamen, plus leading local citizens, also worshipped here in those God-fearing days.

Henry Ginn designed the church in 1840, the year convict transportation to NSW ended officially, although the last of them came nine years later.

The 1844 Garrison Church of the Holy Trinity, steeped in history, at the corner of Argyle and Lower Fort Streets, Millers Point.

The Hero of Waterloo, a Sydney icon like a colonial ale house, and haunted.

Its builder was George Patten. Services began in 1843 in the partly-finished building behind a wall of wood. Additions to the small Gothic Revival church were completed in 1878. Do go inside. The sanctified aura here has a glow of orange from stained-glass windows that reflects from an old pipe organ. The window spaces were first filled with medieval-style oiled canvas. The eastern window was donated by book collector David Scott Mitchell's parents.

It is easy here to imagine a priest in the pulpit addressing some 350 uniformed soldiers and sailors. The Garrison Church remains a popular place of Anglican worship.

The little building beside it, built in 1844 of the sandstone Sydney is so blessed with, and looking older than the church, is the Holy Trinity School building. A student here was knickerbockered Edmund Barton, destined to be knighted and the first Prime Minister of Australia. Now the parish hall, the building's days as a school ended in 1942.

51 Lower Fort Street grew from a track worn by soldiers marching to and from the Dawes Battery. Continue north along this memorable street, lined by intriguing old terrace houses. On the next corner on the left, at the top of Windmill Street, is the plain Regency wedge, **The Hero of Waterloo**. This pub of stone is a favourite of your author, retaining a dignified and spartan flavour of colonial ale houses right down to its old, and working, fireplace. It even has faux or false windows like the former Union Bond Store in Playfair Street at The Rocks (see page 129) made fashionable by Britain's extraordinary window tax.

The Hero is another hotel with claims to a first. Perhaps this is Sydney's oldest pub. It certainly feels so. An illegal sly-grog shop may have been here, but the licence goes back to 1845. George Payton built the Hero a year or two earlier, when convicts were completing Semi-circular Quay and the confinement of the Tank Stream. The hero of Waterloo was, of course, the Duke of Wellington, the conqueror of Napoleon at Waterloo.

The hotel has extensive and eerie stone cellars with convict markings on the walls and an iron-barred cell which once held brawling drunks and, according to legend, young men kidnapped from the bar on behalf of ships' captains needing crew and who, once lugged aboard, awoke at sea. Behind the barred cell is the beginning of a tunnel, which allegedly connected with the little 1829 Shipwrights Arms Inn next door in Windmill Street, now a private residence. The tunnel was said to go all the way, under the Hit or Miss Hotel, to the waterfront at Walsh Bay. It was at least a drain, perhaps also used by smugglers. But the hard rock prevented construction of such tunnels at The Rocks. Millers Point's base is not much different.

Convict chains in the Hero's cellar.

The Rocks and Sydney Cove from Flagstaff Hill in 1800, 12 years after white settlement.
Mitchell Library, State Library of NSW

The ghost of convict Ann Kirkman, who died here dramatically aged 33 in the mid 1800s, is said to haunt the Hero of Waterloo. The persistent poltergeist is blamed for moving chairs and playing the piano in the night, and she is said to dislike men.

A wall in the Hero's bar sports a proclamation of the 1900 Bubonic Plague. It is a popular spot for local (mostly traditional) jazz combos, and even sometimes a troupe of Morris dancers, at weekends. A little more colourful were the names of other public houses in Old Sydney. They included The Black Dog, the Whaler's Arms, the Sailor's Return, the Sheer Hulk, the Brown Bear, the Ship and Mermaid, the Cat and Fiddle and The World Turned Upside Down.

The corner building facing The Hero was licensed in 1842 as The Young Princess grocery shop. It was named after Queen Victoria's eldest daughter, Victoria of Prussia, the mother of Kaiser Bill.

52 Continue our walk back south along the footpath on the western side of Lower Fort Street to exquisite **Argyle Place**, the quality row of Millers Point, with a long line of venerable terrace houses facing a sort of village green punctuated by plane trees, oaks and poplars and often rowdy with squabbling birds.

This was a popular rendezvous spot for military types and the gentry, lit by three gaslight lamps with an 1869 drinking fountain at its Garrison Church end.

Quality Row of elegant terrace houses to the left, trees teeming with birds on the right, at Miller's Point's Argyle Place Park.

53

The Lord Nelson, Sydney's oldest pub at the corner of Argyle and Kent Streets.

53 Stroll west to the corner of Kent Street, where the famous **Lord Nelson Hotel** presides. Now, there is little doubt that this one is Sydney's oldest, continually-operating, hotel and also private brewery, but its notoriously potent, lay 'em out, Nelson's Blood Stout is no longer available. Perhaps just as well, if you want to finish our Walk.

The hotel, still Georgian and austere, has lost most of its colonial edge from when it was licensed in 1838, largely the result of renovations in 1998. Its first landlord and builder was Billy Wells, reckoned to have fought in the sea Battle of Trafalgar. It remains one of the city's more popular drinking holes and dining centres.

The land behind the Lord Nelson falls away abruptly towards the Harbour. This northern end of Kent Street was called Scotch Row (which really should be Scots Row) because a lot of Scottish born people lived here.

James Taylor's drawing of Aborigines camped near Millers Point (right) and Darling Harbour about 1820. Mitchell Library, State Library of NSW.

54 This is not a pub crawl, but perched on an escarpment by the water at the end of Argyle Street is the towering **Palisades Hotel**, built in 1912. The brick Federation premises with recessed balconies on its five floors and featuring the famous old Palisades Restaurant, is near Sydney's earliest quarry.

Whaling and sealing ships anchored in crescent-shaped Walsh Bay from 1790 until about 1840. The sailors blew their pay at pubs, sly grog shops and brothels at The Rocks while cargoes were unloaded and stores were taken to their ships from lighters. The bay takes its name from Henry Deane Walsh, Engineer in Chief of the Sydney Harbour Trust for 18 years from 1901. Finger wharves of Australian timber were built here and worked busily until the 1960s. They were the scene of many fiery strikes by wharfies.

Notoriously colourful Jack the Miller gave this headland its name after it was first called Cockle Bay Point, although the name survives farther along our Walk at Darling Harbour. Jack Leighton built three windmills here from the 1790s to grind mostly flour from grain that arrived on ships moored below in the bay. Jack's pioneering empire prospered despite him declining from Governor Hunter a grant of all the promontory if he would fence it off from the rest of the community.

Jack climbed up a ladder to near the top of one his windmills in 1826 after a drinking binge. He tumbled to his death, drunk, aged 57. Steam mills took over from those driven by the wind in the 1830s. Windmill Street was named so as it was the original route from Jack the Millers' mills to The Rocks.

Part Nine

Millers Point, Darling Harbour, Chinatown

AUSTRALIA'S OLDEST Catholic church, the city's first conjoined cottage, the Hungry Mile, majestic ships, thousands of native animals and water creatures, the nation's biggest museum and the delights of Chinatown are ahead in this final leg of our amble.

55 Cross Argyle Street and stroll south past the Millers Point Post Office on the eastern side of Kent Street. A few doors along here, hard against the footpath at No. 14, is **St. Brigids Catholic School and Church**. This little-known and modest precinct was approved for a place of Catholic worship by Governor Bourke in 1833. Construction began a year later and the church opened in May 1835. It is the oldest surviving place of Catholic worship in Australia, says the sign in front, despite it being closed for a while in the late 1800s. The first Catholic church, at the site of St Marys Cathedral, burned down.

The opening of the main building of blocks of golden local sandstone was an emotional boon for Old Sydney's many Catholics, a lot of them former convicts from Ireland. They had had a hard time practising their religion against some entrenched official bigotry. Some of the colony's first convict priests were not recognised as such by the administration, which at first would not condone Catholic religious ceremonies. The Rev Jeremiah Flynn, for instance, was branded an illegal immigrant from Ireland. The lively cleric was deported about 1818 after hiding at homes of his followers for a year, celebrating Mass for the trusted. Two Catholic priests were finally admitted to the settlement officially two years later.

Chunky St Brigids School and Church in Kent Street, the oldest place of Catholic worship in Australia, following early colonial bigotry against the faith.

Stubbornly marooned on its rocky peak like Noah's craft on Mt Ararat is the oldest stand-alone cottage in Sydney, Glover's Cottage, more commonly known as The Ark.

Long and impressive rows of old timber, brick and stone terrace homes of late Victorian design line both sides of Kent Street, straight as a laser beam below the eastern escarpment of Observatory Hill. Kent Street here also hosts the Observatory Hotel.

Farther along are the historic Agar Steps, cut from the cliff and clothed in greenery. They gave early access to and from the famous lookout. They are named after Thomas Agar, a settler here in 1829 and designed by Sydney City Engineer Edward Ball. The Victorian Italianate terrace houses facing the steps were erected from the 1870s to 1880s.

The Agar Steps' connection to the then high meadow where soldiers sometimes exercised caused this street to be named Soldiers Row before Governor Macquarie, the all-time champion at naming places after himself, his family and Britain's leaders, rebranded it with the name of Queen Victoria's dissolute father, Prince Edward, the Duke of Kent. The steps also gave handy access to the colonial military hospital and the Fort Street High School.

Gabled 1850 Richmond Villa is the two-storey building of sandstone a little south at 120 Kent Street. Busy Colonial Architect Mortimer Lewis built the villa and lived in it for a few years on its original site facing the Domain behind the Parliamentary buildings in Macquarie Street until it was taken, brick by brick, to this suburban perch.

56 Next door, on a shelf of rock, is Glover's Cottage, widely known as **The Ark**. In the early 1820s, some years after John Dickson's steam engine brought the Industrial Revolution to Sydney, stonemason Thomas Glover built the ancient-looking block and two others on the ledge, given to him by an indulgent Governor Macquarie. One cottage collapsed and the other was demolished when Kent Street was cut through Glover's property. That left The Ark marooned high, dry and alone as if on a little Mount Ararat. The author understands the plain and solid cottage of oddball rock was Sydney's first semi-detached cottage.

It will remain protected on its domain long after the new towers that block The Ark's views have been replaced. This ends abruptly the old residential part of Kent Street, the southern section of which was called The Quarries, providing stone for buildings near and far.

57 To get to another part of Old Sydney, turn right into Gas Lane to confront the lesser side of the headquarters of the **Australian Gas Light Company**, a venerable old building that faces Hickson Road several levels below. Streets were first lit by gas lights provided and fuelled from this sandstone centre from May 1841, the year before Sydney was declared a city, although a few shops had had gas lighting as a novelty for some years.

Gas gradually replaced street lamps burning whale oil that had been in the heart of the settlement since the first of them shone a yellowish glow over Macquarie Place, Bridge Street, in 1826. When gas lighting came to Sydney, a newspaper enthused that it was "the first in the Asiatic world to have this beautiful art, this exquisite production of science".

Continue our Walk to the right, or northern, end of the AGL building of offices and a verandahed restaurant with sublime views over Darling Harbour, Pyrmont and Balmain. Go down a long and steep flight of steps here to Hickson Road, from where we can take in the augustness of the home of gas lighting for the nation. The one floor we confronted at the top of the building is the top of five levels from here. The pink brick building next door, to the south, was built in 1899, the year troops sailed from Sydney to the Boer War, as the AGL Company's Carburetted Water Gas plant. Water gas, of all things, was found to be more efficient for lighting than coal gas, burning much hotter and brighter.

In the hard days of unemployment in the late 1920s and early 1930s Depression, with hundreds of men desperately looking for work here, the mile (1.6 km) of wharves along Hickson Road was known as The Hungry Mile.

The wharves at Darling Harbour, showing the Australian Gas Light Co., about 1870. Mitchell Library, State Library of NSW.

SNAPSHOT 1930
A bridge monkey remembers that Hungry Mile

THIS IS TERRIFYING! My first day on the job and they've put me way up here. If I am still alive at the end of the day, could I just go back to walking the Hungry Mile? Oh, no, John. I wonder how Ernest Antony thought of that title for his poem? A mate told me that Ernie was one of us on Hickson Street. How else could he capture the emotions we all had?

They tramp there in their legions on the mornings dark and cold, To beg the right to slave for bread from Sydney's lords of gold. They toil and sweat in slavery, 'twould make the devil smile To see the Sydney wharfies tramping down the hungry mile.

If only the 'lords of gold' could be in our threadbare shoes; even for a day. And feel the depression of constant rejection. Comprehend the grief of hunger and the despair that fills the heart when you return empty-handed to the wife and kids. If they could see the looks on the little ones' faces when they know they will have only scraps again for dinner. But what really cuts hard is when the wife says, "There now, John, things will be better tomorrow, you'll see." It tears my heart out. She knows things will not get better; she's trying to cheer me up. I feel like hiding under the bedcovers and giving up on life. Yes 'Sydney's lords of gold', I wonder how you would cop that.

But things have just changed. I have a job. For a few months, at least, so long as I keep my footing. I'm holding on for grim death perched hundreds of metres over Sydney Harbour helping to build this massive bridge. As each steel member is lifted into place, my job is to tighten the temporary bolts before the rivets are driven home.

The bolts have to be tight. I apply all the strength I can muster to the long lever attached to the spanner. Twice this morning the spanner slipped off and I lost my balance, teetering at the edge. But when I arrive home today I will be the bread winner. I will have their respect again. Soon, they will eat aplenty. No more Hungry Mile.

Pyrmont Bridge teemed with traffic the day the toll was removed in August 1884.

58 Just a little farther along are the steps to the old **Pyrmont Bridge**, now a scenic pedestrian walk across Cockle Bay under the monorail. It has a lively history.

A private company opened a low, wooden bridge here on St Patrick's Day in 1858 as a much-needed short cut to growing Balmain to the west. It charged a toll of two pence a person and a farthing (a quarter of a penny) a head for livestock, which we assume included colonials' horses, dogs and cats.
An opening central span allowed ships to pass through.

Then in 1884 the Government bought the bridge and abolished the toll. It was suddenly crammed with travellers, including delivery carts and herded sheep and cattle. They previously had to go many kilometres south around the bay to avoid paying the toll.

A higher bridge on pylons of sandstone was opened in 1902 to become the main route west out of the city. The Pyrmont Bridge closed to vehicles in 1981. Spared from demolition, it was declared a National Engineering Landmark in 1992.

We get a fine view of Darling Harbour and its surrounds strolling over the bridge, which has a detailed map displayed half way across. To the right are some gracious old ladies of the sea, the splendid replica of Cook's *Endeavour*, the 1878 square rigger *James Craig*, the former Navy destroyer *Vampire*, the Oberon class submarine *Onslow*, the little hero commando raider of World War II *Krait*, the former Manly ferry *South Steyne* which your author commuted on for years, and beyond, the bright red former lighthouse ship *Carpentaria*. The old girls are usually open for our inspection.

59 At the end of the bridge, take the steps to the right to visit the Australian National Maritime Museum behind huge Admiralty-pattern anchors from the 1839 merchant vessel *Vernon*, destroyed by fire in 1893 after spending years moored at Cockatoo Dock as a training school for young sailors.

The museum has been a magnet for anyone with a nautical bent, like your oldish-salt author, since it opened in 1991. Massive displays on different levels showcase the history of maritime Australia, including the first Australians, the Aborigines. Regular guided tours show off the lot. The museum's high walls and diving roof were designed to accommodate the masts of boats exhibited. An amazing number of fine model craft are on sale, along with books and souvenirs, in the museum's big shop.

We recommend that you leave the museum from its northern side to have a good look at, perhaps go on board, the ships moored around here and also examine a big and growing Welcome Wall. It lists the names of thousands of settlers from more than 100 nations who forged this nation. You can add their names if you have any immigrant pioneer ancestors. More information is on www.anmm.gov.au/ww

The Admiralty-pattern anchors from the burned hulk of Vernon beside the National Maritime Museum.

By the jetties here on our latest visit, your author saw shoals of half-kilo (pan size) fish that looked like bream. Another sure sign, that was, of a Harbour recovering its pristine health.

Stroll south in front of the Maritime Museum beside the bay, by snack bars and a water taxi ramp. After going under the Pyrmont Bridge, we have the choice of continuing beside the water or reconnecting with

59

The replica of Captain Cook's HMS Endeavour defies the city skyline at Darling Harbour.

Darling Harbour has changed mightily since this photo was taken in 1967. Mitchell Library, State Library of NSW.

A WALK IN OLD SYDNEY

it after going through a modern arcade to the right full of restaurants and shops selling all sorts of things.

60 Birds, notably ibis, pigeons and gulls, are thick around the rest of our Walk south-east by fountains and artificial waterways. Continue under busy motorways to **Darling Harbour's Visitor Centre**, packed with books and free brochures about various attractions. Staff here know about current attractions and can show you how to find various destinations or accommodation.

The vast apartment buildings to the west were once wool stores. The nearby suburbs of Ultimo, Balmain and Glebe were rough and tough parts of Old Sydney with shanty houses, factories and storehouses. They are trendy and chic parts of town today. The former Pyrmont Powerhouse, for instance, is now the Star City casino complex.

A WALK IN OLD SYDNEY

60

A lake and gulls on the lawn at Darling Harbour abut a terrace of towers east in the city.

61 Darling Harbour has many places of interest. One we recommend for a reflective break is the remarkable **Chinese Garden**, only a few minutes' walk south of the Visitor Centre. This sole authentic Chinese garden outside Asia covering 2.4 hectares was a gift to the Australian people by the citizens of Guangdong Province, a sister State to NSW. The gift marked the Bicentenary of white settlement at Sydney Cove. It is quite another world of shimmering ponds, waterfalls, wind bells, traditional carvings, a bonsai nursery, bamboo and grasses beside pathways of stone and a teahouse.

62 Nor should we miss, a fair walk on an elevated path to the west, the spectacular and vast **Powerhouse Museum**. It is Australia's biggest museum, on the site of a 1902 tram depot and the Ultimo Power Station. Some of the station's machinery here is still in working order. This treasure house displays more than 400,000 objects acquired over 125 years. They include examples of the decorative arts, Australian history, fashion, design, transport, science and technology, plus items relating to outer space. Zoe's House and Cogs' Playground are interactive play centres for children. The museum, with regular guided tours, is open every day except Christmas Day.

You can catch a water taxi or ferry from Darling Harbour back to Circular

The enticing Chinese Garden, the sole authentic one outside Asia, a gift from the people of the NSW sister state in China, Guangdong.

Quay. Or take the monorail to the heart of the city, a short stroll from the Hyde Park Barracks, from where we set out on this adventure.

Two Old Sydney architectural icons you should see in the CBD some time, which our horse-shoe route skirted around, are the City of Sydney Town Hall and the glorious Queen Victoria Building, both where Park Street crosses George Street.

63 But, meantime, we have a better option! Go to the southern end of Darling Harbour and take a five-minute walk south in Day Street, then left on Liverpool Street into Dixon Street, the heart of marvellous **Chinatown**. This is where we should celebrate the completion of our Walk with liquid refreshment, yum cha or a dish from the finest cuisine in the world. That's what your author does.

As we reported while there, The Rocks was the first hub for Sydney's vibrant Chinese community. Most of them moved here to the Haymarket, the raw home of the city's busy fruit, vegetable, meat and fish markets, in the 1890s. Bustling Chinatown is a colourful Oriental metropolis in the heart of a big city with hundreds of restaurants, herbalists and vendors of exotic foods, utensils and clothes. Your author remembers here and there the mysterious doors of joss houses and gambling and opium dens. But it has always been a fairly law-abiding place. The restaurants serve dishes from all of China's regions.

Dixon Street, with stone dragons at decorated old portals at each end, becomes a cauldron of celebrations on the night of the first full moon after every January 21. It marks China's New Year. Fireworks and beating drums accompany dragon dancers and relatives giving children red packets of coins. All around is the cry, Kong Hee Fat Choy – wishing you prosperity.

YOUR AUTHOR HOPES YOU are more enlightened, fitter and even lighter after walking the Walk in Old Sydney whether you did it in a few hours or, shopping or dining or gently taking liquid replenishment along the way, a few days. Reward yourself. As Mike Tatlow did, raise a congratulatory glass in Chinatown. Cheers!

Further Reading

When preparing this book, your author found the following books to be fine research aids and thanks the authors and publishers and recommend their books for further reading.

Brodsky, Isadore. *Heart of The Rocks*. Sydney 1965.

Cossu, Anna. (Historic Houses Trust of NSW) *A Place in The Rocks*. Sydney 2007.

Fitzgerald, Shirley. *Sydney 1842-1992*. Sydney 1992.

Karskens, Grace. *The Rocks. Life in early Sydney*. Melbourne 1992.

Kelly, Max. Anchored in a Small Cove. *A history and archaeology of The Rocks, Sydney*. Sydney 1997.

Park, Ruth. Ruth Park's *Sydney*. Sydney 1999.

Sharpe, Alan. Pictorial *History City of Sydney*. Sydney 2005.

Smith, Keith and Irene. *Smith's Guide to Sydney City*. Sydney 1988.

Turnbull, Lucy Hughes. *Sydney. Biography of a city*. Sydney 1999.

Acknowledgements

I would like to thank Brian McDonald, a significant contributor and back-stop checker for historical accuracy, who has a refreshing eye for the odd and comic side of our history and is a tour guide with The Rocks Walking Tours. I am particularly grateful to Brian for contributing the 'Snapshots' that appear throughout the book. Contributions and valued guidance also came from Dr Wayne Johnson, Archaeologist and Curator of The Rocks Discovery Museum, Sydney Harbour Foreshore Authority. Important helpers were Tasmanian historian Peter Mercer OAM, our co-author of *A Tour of Old Tasmania*. Our thanks also go to the Hyde Park Barracks Museum, the Historic Houses Trust of NSW, the Museum of Sydney, the Mitchell Library, the National Trust of Australia (NSW), history buffs Norma and Melissa Holmes, Olive Lonergan, Paul Denham and Michael Johnson. Special thanks also to leading Australian journalist, broadcaster, fellow author and friend, Charles Wooley.

The Rocks tour guide and contributor to this book, Brian McDonald, telling visitors about Cadman's Cottage.

Shopping 1890s-style at the Cheap Cash Grocer's shop, Susannah Place

From left: Once a year, Hyde Park Barracks staff dress in authentic costumes and perform duties from the era. Charles Wooley and Michael Tatlow look on as convicts leave Hyde Park Barracks for a day's work under the guard of a Red Coat soldier; as in the early 1800s.

About the Author

MICHAEL TATLOW has lived and worked in Sydney, the city he loves, for many years as a freelance journalist, Chief of Staff of *The Daily Telegraph* and News Editor of *The Sunday Telegraph* and *The Bulletin*. He later headed ABC-TV News and Current Affairs in Tasmania, where he became an ardent fly-fisher of trout.

Now an acknowledged historian, he has written the best-sellers *A Walk in Old Hobart*, *A Walk in Old Launceston* and *A Tour of Old Tasmania*.

Michael's ancestors, including convicts, came to Australia from Ireland in the 1820s. He began his career as a reporter with a newspaper in Tasmania after making a living fishing for shark and trapping rabbits. He has a son and daughter, and six grandchildren.

Other related titles by New Holland Publishers

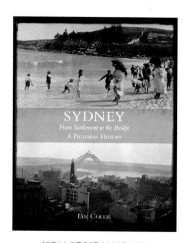

ISBN 9781741105209

ISBN 9781876334291

ISBN 9781742570235

Published in Australia in 2011 by
New Holland Publishers (Australia) Pty Ltd
Sydney • Auckland • London • Cape Town

1/66 Gibbes Street Chatswood NSW 2067 Australia
218 Lake Road Northcote Auckland New Zealand
86 Edgware Road London W2 2EA United Kingdom
80 McKenzie Street Cape Town 8001 South Africa

www.newholland.com.au

A record of this book is held at the National Library of Australia

ISBN 9781742571973

Publisher: Fiona Schultz
Publishing Manager: Lliane Clarke
Project Editor: Bronwyn Phillips
Designer: Kimberley Pearce
Production Manager: Olga Dementiev
Printer: Toppan Leefung Printing Ltd (China)

10 9 8 7 6 5 4 3 2 1

Keep up with New Holland Publishers on
Facebook http://www.facebook.com/NewHollandPublishers and
Twitter @NewHollandAU